Naming Rumpelstiltskin

WHO WILL PROFIT AND WHO
WILL LOSE IN THE WORKPLACE
OF THE 21ST CENTURY

Ann Finlayson

KEY PORTER  BOOKS

Canadian Cataloguing in Publication Data

Finlayson, Ann, 1941–

             Naming Rumpelstiltskin : who will profit and who will lose
             in the workplace of the 21st century

ISBN 1-55013-763-8

1. Work – Social aspects. 2. Work environment – Social aspects.
3. Employees – Effect of technological innovations on. I. Title.

HD4904.F55 1996   306.3'6   C96-930895-7

The publisher gratefully acknowledges the assistance of the Canada Council and the Ontario Arts Council.

Key Porter Books Limited
70 The Esplanade
Toronto, Ontario
Canada M5E 1R2

Printed and bound in Canada

96 97 98 99 6 5 4 3 2 1

Matthew, Stephanie, Abigail and Simon, Brigid and Joel
—This one's for you

Contents

Acknowledgements

First and foremost, I want to thank the many young people (especially my nephew, Matthew Aitchison) who shared with me the details of their working lives, their concerns about their futures, and their hopes for better times to come. May their awesome resilience and resourcefulness keep them afloat in a roiling sea of workplace troubles.

I am grateful to Susan Renouf, for allowing me to deliver to Key Porter a very different book from the one I promised her, and for delivering to me the perfect editor, Charis Wahl, whose constant good humour, enthusiasm for the project, and superb editing skills made a difficult task fun. Their faith in me was a welcome delight.

Several friends whose expertise and views I value highly agreed to read all or part of the manuscript. Bill Nelson's comments, especially on the potentially catastrophic environmental consequences of globalization, were invaluable, as were Allan Shapira's thoughts on pension matters (although I doubt that he would want to be too closely associated with this book). Norman Zacour, as always, made me think twice about issues large and small, although I'm still not persuaded, as he is, that "societal" is nothing more than an uppity way of saying "social."

Susan Beattie provided me with valuable insights into what is happening in our high schools, especially in large urban schools trying to meet ever-growing challenges with ever-diminishing resources. Linda Bailey's unpublished work on pay equity issues was also extremely useful to me, as were Mona Kornberg's insights into the challenges of downsizing and privatizing in the public sector. Trish Shorter proved to me that it is possible not only to meet the heavy demands of a traditional corporate job at home, but also to do so with grace and efficiency, in the company of a one-year-old. Jack McLeod persuaded me that a closer acquaitanceship with the economic theories of Joseph Schumpeter is not a bad thing to have, and Charles Tilly gave me a knowledgeable and insightful overview of the current debate over workplace change in the United States. He also directed me to recent academic studies I might otherwise have overlooked, including Chris Tilly's ground-breaking work on corporate policies and the changing U.S. labour market. I want too to thank Jan Whitford, for her customary efficiency and steady encouragement; David Kilgour, for his help and enthusiasm when I was in the early stages of developing this book; and Janice Weaver and Beverley Endersby, for their help in the later stages.

I am, as always, deeply grateful to my husband, Michael, who, although he is far too sweet to say so, also may wish not to be too closely associated with this book. I thank him for his never-ending support, his interest, and his clarity of vision. I also want to reassure him that nobody but a Rumpelstiltskin—and certainly nobody who knows us—would ever expect us to agree on everything.

Finally, I want to pay my respects to all those who have written carefully and humanely, in research studies, books, and articles of their own, about the many pressing issues raised in this book. Because *Naming Rumpelstiltskin* is above all a book about ideas, about alternatives, and about the critical importance of informed debate in a democratic society, there is no way it could have been written without them.

The Tale of Rumpelstiltskin

Once upon a time there was a poor miller who had a beautiful daughter. It came to pass that this miller had cause to call upon the King on a matter of business. Wishing to appear important, the miller said to the King, "It may interest Your Majesty to know that I have a daughter who can spin straw into gold."

"This is an art that interests me indeed," said the King. "If your daughter is truly as clever as you say she is, bring her to my palace tomorrow so that I may try her unusual talent."

When the girl was brought to him, the King took her into a room filled with straw. He led her to a spinning-wheel, handed her a bobbin, and said, "Now you must set to work. If, by tomorrow morning early, you have not spun this straw into gold, you must die."

Then he locked the door, leaving her in the room alone.

The miller's daughter, having no idea how to spin straw into gold, stared at the spinning-wheel, growing ever more miserable. Finally, she began to weep.

Suddenly, the door opened and in came a strange little man. "Good evening," he said. "Why do you cry so piteously?"

"Alas," replied the girl, "I must spin this straw into gold before the morning and I do not know how to do it."

"What will you give me," asked the little man, "if I do it for you?"

"My necklace," said the miller's daughter.

The little man took the necklace. Then he sat down in front of the wheel. Turn, turn, turn, three times, and the bobbin was full. Turn, turn, turn, and a second bobbin was full. And so it went— turn, turn, turn, all night long, until all the straw was spun and all the bobbins were full of gold.

The King arrived at daybreak. When he saw the gold, he was delighted, but his heart became even more greedy. He led the miller's daughter to another, larger, room. It too was full of straw.

"If you value your life, you will spin this straw into gold before daybreak," he said, and locked her in the room.

Again, the girl began to cry. Again, the door opened and the little man appeared before her.

"What will you give me if I help you again?" he asked.

"The ring on my finger," she answered.

The little man snatched the ring. Then he sat down in front of the wheel and began to spin. By daybreak, turn, turn, turn, he had spun all the straw into shining gold.

The King rejoiced at the sight of the gold, but he still had not gold enough. He led the miller's daughter into an even larger room full of straw.

"Tonight, you must spin this straw into gold," he said. "But when you have completed your task, your labours will be over and you shall be my wife."

Though she be only a miller's daughter, thought the King, she is very pretty, and I could not find a richer wife were I to search the world over.

The miller's daughter looked around the huge room stuffed with straw. Not even the little man, she thought, could help her this time.

But help he did. "What will you give me if I spin this straw into gold for you?" he asked.

"I have nothing left to give," she replied sadly.

"Then promise me that if you become Queen, you will give me your first-born child."

The miller's daughter looked around the huge room stuffed with straw. At first she hesitated. Then she said to herself, How can I know that the King speaks the truth? How can I know that I shall be his wife? How can I know that there ever will be a child?

So she promised, and the little man spun the straw into gold.

When the King arrived at daybreak and found that his bidding had been done, he took her hand in marriage and the miller's daughter became Queen.

A year later, she bore a beautiful child, and never did she give a thought to the strange little man. But suddenly he appeared. "Give me what you promised," he demanded.

The Queen was filled with horror and offered the little man all the riches of the kingdom instead.

But the little man refused. "I have no need of your treasures," he said. "You promised me your child."

The Queen began to weep, and the little man took pity on her. "I will give you three days," he said. "If in that time you discover my name, you shall keep your child."

All night long, the Queen lay awake, thinking of all the names she had ever heard. When the little man appeared the next day, she began with Caspar, Melchior, Balthazar—all the names she knew, one after the other. But to every one, the little man said, "That is not my name."

The next day, the Queen sent messengers throughout the land, seeking other names. That night she repeated to the little man the strangest of them. "Perhaps your name is Bandylegs, or Crooked Back, or Long Nose." But he always answered, "That is not my name."

On the third day, a messenger returned and said, "I have not discovered a single new name, but I did witness a strange sight. In the forest, I saw a little house. In front of the house a fire was burning. Round and round the fire, a strange little man was leaping about, singing a strange little song:

Today I brew, tomorrow I bake.
The next, the young Queen's child I'll take,
How glad I am that neither man nor dame
Knows Rumpelstiltskin is my name.

How happy the Queen was when she heard that name! But when the little man returned, and demanded to know if she had discovered him, she pretended to be worried.

"Is your name Conrad?" she asked?

"No," he answered.

"Is your name Barnabas?"

"No," he answered.

"Perhaps, then, your name is Rumpelstiltskin?"

"The Devil told you that! The Devil told you that!" the little man cried. In his rage, he plunged his right foot deep into the ground. Then he pulled so hard at his left leg with both his hands that he tore himself in two.

And thus it was that Rumpelstiltskin was no more.

Introduction
The Rumpelstiltskin Factor

The nineties have been wrenching times for Canadians, and nowhere have the dislocations been greater than in the workplace, a world turned upside down by forces seemingly beyond our control. Where once there were jobs, there are none. Where once there was security, there is flux. Where once there was optimism, there is fear. In addition to the human misery of unemployment, the absence of "jobs, jobs, jobs" is generating societal anxiety, endless reportage—and, so far, few concrete solutions. Nearly half a decade after the demoralizing recession of the early nineties ended "officially," we are still searching for a way out of our difficulties.

Virtually without exception, the experts who write about the jobs crisis cite radical changes in the way we work—and in the work to be done—as the primary cause of the problem. Virtually without exception, they portray Canadians as pawns in a global economic upheaval. Pick up any newspaper, and you will find at least one op-ed piece on the employment crisis. Go to any bookstore and you will find books that seek to persuade us that technology is the answer to our problems or, conversely, that technology is the cause of our problems. Turn on your television, and you will see people talking dispiritedly about the lack of jobs.

All these discussions share two assumptions: first, that technology is the force that is driving workplace change; and, second, that we have no choice but to accept this change and adapt to its inevitable consequences. Recovery, so far as it has taken place, has been largely jobless, we are told, because new computerized information technologies, in the context of the globalization of trade, have caused fundamental structural change in our economy. Structural change, in turn, has led to massive lay-offs, wage reductions, benefit take-backs, bankruptcies, and the creation of few jobs except "bad" ones. We are not alone, the argument goes. All industrialized Western societies are coping with unemployment and none has found the answer.

There can be no question that technology *is* changing the way we work and that global competition *is* forcing corporations to re-examine the way they do business. Nor can there be any question that the need to contain deficits has obliged governments to rethink the way they spend taxpayers' money, a reassessment that has led to the elimination of both jobs and services. But the grim determinism that has characterized the debate about jobs and joblessness is not serving us well. Not only has it paralysed us with fear, causing us to abandon efforts to find better ways to work, but it has also prevented us from asking hard and necessary questions about the motives of those who enthusiastically preach the gospel of ruthless workplace change. For, by stressing the inevitability of change, they have persuaded us that there are no choices to be made, no real decisions to be taken.

When I began to research this book more than two years ago, my intention was straightforward: to examine the way work is changing as we approach the twenty-first century, with a particular emphasis on the implications of these changes for younger Canadians. Its genesis was my concern and puzzlement about what seemed to be happening under my own roof. Watching our family—six young adults, five of them over age twenty—struggle with the new workplace was an effective, and troubling, wake-up call.

As a group, these young people were remarkably competent, adequately educated, and not unambitious. Yet their prospects seemed to be declining fast. Fully deployed, we could muster a lawyer trying to reconcile a fledgling career with marriage and familial ambitions and responsibilities; an aspiring combatant in the global marketplace, yearning, as he embarked on an M.B.A. program, for a swift return to the excesses of the eighties; a bartender at a historic Toronto pub who finds great satisfaction in the work he does and bridles when it is suggested that it is a "job," not a "career"; an only partially reconstructed Marxist who believes that her graduate work in philosophy and cultural studies will lead to both a job and a higher understanding of life; a waitress and perennial undergraduate who has read more good novels than I ever have and writes better prose than I ever will; and a bright, thoughtful eighteen-year-old, watching the others with curiosity, confusion, and mounting apprehension.

Who, among these intelligent, hard-working, agreeable young adults, I wondered, is catching up with whom? Who is productive and who is not? How does one weigh eight years spent earning a B.A. and a law degree against a satisfying, moderately well-paid job begun at age eighteen? How does one weigh a low-paying job that demands little emotional energy but makes time for the reading—and perhaps, one day, the writing—of good books against a potentially high-paying job that demands an impossibly heavy commitment of time and emotional energy? Which of them is "ahead"? Which of them will "prosper"? Which of them will be "happy" and how much will that happiness depend upon their work? How would you counsel the eighteen-year-old? Is it harder for them than it was for us? How do we measure our answers?

Those were some of the questions I set out to answer, and that was the book I set out to write. In many ways it is the book I have written; but, along the way, I became increasingly uneasy about my task. It seemed to me that my research was going around in ever-widening circles, trapped in a prevailing mind-set that sometimes seemed to defy both logic and sense. In the context of a recession that would not go away, some of my questions seemed to fall outside the current debate over the future of work.

The paradigms I was encountering in my reading and discussions excluded many of the issues that were important to me. My questions seemed to be considered frivolous, outmoded, or simply inappropriate in the economy of the nineties. In short, the paradigms seemed to preclude discussion of many of the workplace issues that seemed both important and entirely relevant to me, and, I think, to most Canadians, as recently as five years ago.

My unease was heightened by a growing suspicion that not all those participating in the debate on jobs and workplace change had declared their full interest in the matter. Is it possible, I wondered, that the debate is only partly about the future of work? Is there more to it? Why, for example, had the most recent recession apparently caused our preoccupations and our goals to change so dramatically, when previous recessions had strengthened our resolve to move forward humanely on such workplace issues as equity, safety, and environmental sensitivity?

Why was no one addressing such questions as the appropriate role of employers in reconciling profits with the interests of their employees and of the society in which they do business? Why had everyone stopped talking about the obvious and urgent need for better, more affordable child care? Why did everyone assume that unions had become historical artifacts, and that the search for a creative working relationship between employers and unions was now passé? Why didn't concerns for equity or for the environment seem to matter anymore?

Moreover, much of the current debate seemed curiously short-sighted. Why, given Canada's striking demographic profile, for example, was no one talking about the need for more flexible ways to organize our working lives in order to accommodate both young and old? Why had we abandoned discussions of the value of unpaid work in the home and in the volunteer sector? Why is the term "welfare state," with all its negative connotations, now used to describe the social programs that not so long ago we agreed were among our proudest achievements as a society?

Most particularly, I became curious about why so many corporate spokespeople, especially those representing large organizations, had so eagerly embraced the theories of those who tell us that the "job" is dead, the "career" extinct. Why were they so keen to "outsource" and "right-size" people out of jobs, so certain that in the past they had given their employees too much money and too many benefits? The world truly had been turned upside down in less than a decade; everyone writing about the changes could see the inevitability and desirability of the new order, except me.

Corporate apologists seemed far too eager to embrace technologically determinist explanations of workplace change. Often, their enthusiasm seemed unwarranted, their rhetoric overblown, their analyses exaggerated. The very language they used seemed to be borrowed from the technologies they were so quick to embrace: "re-engineering," "restructuring," "downsizing."

Of course technology is changing the way we work, I found myself thinking, but technology—at different rates at different times—has always changed the way people work. *Of course* some kinds of jobs are disappearing, but jobs have always disappeared, to be replaced by other kinds of jobs. By one estimate, since the Second World War, eight thousand occupations have disappeared and more than six thousand have been created. *Of course* we need to prepare ourselves and our children for the jobs of tomorrow; but we have always adapted our skills to new technologies. Why would we not do so today?

The complaints of the corporate community that Canadians are reluctant to embrace the technology of the information age, for example, struck me as nonsense. Most Canadians now use computers in their work or in their homes, or both, and university students take it for granted that the computer is an essential tool with which to pursue knowledge and a degree. When it becomes necessary, all but the most perverse of us have learned how to use a computer, just as we have learned to use automated teller machines, voice mail, fax machines, and VCRs. We don't all learn to build a computer or to program or repair one (although many of us do learn these skills), but with almost a quarter of Canadian households now accessing the Internet, most of us have at least some computer knowledge and are eager to acquire more.

Similarly, most Canadians, when asked, readily agree that there are better systems for organizing our working lives than the one we have now. Many of us, for example, say we would be happy to have a shorter work week, even if it means earning less money, just as many of us say we are prepared to forgo paid overtime if it creates jobs for others. It simply doesn't make sense to many Canadians that some of us routinely work twenty hours' overtime each week while others are not working at all. These and other ideas for recasting how we work were not radical a decade ago; they were not radical two decades ago. They seem, however, to have become radical in the nineties.

This book is an attempt to sort out why these shifts in

perspectives have occurred, and, particularly, why they have occurred at this time. How could our assumptions, and our dreams for our own and our children's futures, have undergone such radical, and dismal, transformations in little more than five years? Why have we come to believe that there are no choices that can be made, no decisions that can be taken, to benefit us, both as individuals and as one of the richest, most envied societies in the world? Why have we passively bought into such a destructive mind-set?

Might the jobs crisis be driven as much by ideological fervour and narrow self-interest as by technology and globalization? Are there those who have a stake, direct or indirect, in keeping unemployment high? In short, *are* there those who think Canada *ought* to become more like the United States, where the widening gap between "good" jobs and "bad" jobs is bifurcating society alarmingly?

As I attempted to find answers to these questions, I found it extremely helpful to ask two simple questions, no matter the specific topic—who, if anyone, is likely to benefit from the changes in question? and who, if anyone, is likely to lose?—and then to ponder whether those who declare change to be inevitable have been completely upfront about their motives and interests.

If they have not, it seemed to me to be my obligation to say so, even though this obligation changed substantially the focus of the book I had intended to write. For it had become clear to me that there are Rumpelstiltskins in our midst, self-interested proponents of workplace change who purport to help us by making us offers that we should— and can—refuse.

These Rumpelstiltskins are demanding, in the name of profit and ideology, that our social programs be dismantled, that our universities and schools be devoted to meeting their needs, that our environmental-protection and workplace-safety laws be denatured, that all our contri-

butions to the Canada Pension Plan be redirected into capital markets, and a lot more too. In their indifference to
high rates of unemployment, they are also trying to steal
our first-borns by creating a permanent pool of disposable
workers, workers who will never enjoy job security, or
opportunities for advancement, or pension plans and benefits, or decent wages.

Until we can name the Rumpelstiltskins, and let the sun
shine brightly on their motives, what hope do we have, as
individuals and as a society, of preserving the progress we
have made and of safeguarding our dreams? How, indeed,
can we even know what, if any, dreams we must abandon
because we truly cannot afford them, or because we are living at a time, and in a world, in which they cannot possibly
come true?

This sceptical approach will cause some Rumpelstiltskins
to call me a conspiracy theorist—a charge not entirely
groundless. I *do* believe in conspiracies of the cynical, conspiracies of the powerful, conspiracies of the self-interested
who deliberately seek, through fear-mongering, or simply
by throwing their weight around, to further their fortunes
at the expense of others.

Corporations do not "conspire." The executives who run
them are simply maximizing profits with little regard for
the societies in which they operate. When those executives
band together in organizations that seek to weaken or over-
turn the limitations society has placed upon their corporate
activities, however, their actions may fairly be called conspiracies, and we would be foolish indeed not to examine
their shared motives and methods.

The recession of the early nineties, which obscured our
perceptions of the differences between normal cyclical
change and irreversible structural change in the workplace, provided the perfect camouflage for a conspiracy of
modern-day Rumpelstiltskins, armed with trickle-down
theories and urgent desires for profit, to roam the world
freely in search of advantageous deals.

When the King is willing to believe that straw can be spun into gold; when the miller is willing to tell a blatant untruth and to risk his daughter's life in order to gain business advantage with the King; when the miller's daughter is so desperate that she pledges her first-born to a shady stranger who presents himself as her salvation—these are dangerous and unnerving times. Yet, even so, there is hope. Deep in his market-driven soul, Rumpelstiltskin felt the faint stirrings of a rudimentary conscience.

Part 1

Chapter 1
The Prosperous Nation
and the Fatal Flaw

"It may interest Your Majesty to know that I have a daughter who can spin straw into gold," said the miller.

"This is an art that interests me indeed," said the King.

Let us, for a moment, consider the King. Perhaps he was a greedy man, vain and uncaring, with a passion for fine china and fast cars. Perhaps he was a gentle, compassionate man, needing gold to assuage the troubles of his subjects. Perhaps he was a giddy, foolish man, overcome by the prospect of wealth beyond measure. Or perhaps he was simply an honest man trying to solve a problem.

Let us imagine that this is a King benign and generous—so generous that his kingdom, though rich in resources and blessed with a cheerful, industrious populace, languishes on the brink of ruin. The kingdom, alas, is in debt to lenders from afar, and the King is short of the ready. No longer can he provide the comforts his subjects have come to take as rightfully theirs. No longer can he be their benefactor. No longer can he keep them safe.

Something must be done. But the people of the realm have little work to do, and the King cannot imagine how they will provide for themselves while he turns his attention to the discharging of the debt. In the absence of his benefaction, will the kingdom fall into disorder and decay? In the absence of his succour, will the citizens sink into despair?

What is a benign and generous King to do? First, it is clear, he must find ways to spend less, dispense fewer benefactions, assuage fewer troubles. Then, he must find ways to raise some cash in order to discharge his debts. Finally, he must harden his heart to the sufferings of his people, for their own good. Perhaps his ministrations to them have been misguided. Perhaps he has been too generous. Perhaps he misunderstood their needs, caused their despair. Now he must seek relief, wherever he can find it.

Imagine, then, the King's joy when the miller appears before him. Imagine his jubilation when he learns of the miller's daughter, who can spin straw into gold. Imagine the intensity of his interest when the miller tells him that the world beyond the kingdom is resplendent with straw, ready to be spun into gold, if only he would engage him to go forth and seek it.

Imagine that!

"There are two kinds of economists," the venerable Harvard economist John Kenneth Galbraith once observed; "those who don't know the future, and those who don't know they don't know." When it comes to the future of work in the short term, we can only hope that he is right, for according to most economists, the chances of a satisfactory resolution to Canada's current job crisis are slim to none in this century. The unemployment rate, they tell us, will not fall much below 9 per cent; joblessness and underemployment will continue to be the norm for young Canadians; and jobs will continue to disappear.

When it comes to the kinds of work we will do in the next century, however, economists know a great deal, although they disagree about what it all means. They know that many of the events that will determine the job market of the twenty-first century have already occurred, and that many of the technological advances that will define the nature of work already exist. Some of these advances, such as fibre-optic networks, are in the early stages of developing their potential; others are as familiar and highly evolved as the computer on your desk. They also know that the way we work is changing more rapidly than at any point in our lifetimes.

To comprehend what has happened to work in Canada in the nineties—and to understand how dramatic transformations in the workplace relate to our current unemployment crisis—it is helpful to consider the broad thrust of changing work patterns over the course of our history. Our evolution from an agrarian society into an urban, industrialized, trade-oriented nation was a rapid one. Between 1896 and 1914, resource-rich Canada enjoyed an export and investment boom that would radically transform the country's economy. As burgeoning new industries—chemicals and electrical equipment, pulp and paper, automobiles and aluminum—pushed Canada into the wider world, they also provided an abundance of new jobs.

As a result, except during of the prolonged and painful years of the Great Depression, a sharp recession in the early eighties, and two or three less damaging economic downturns, Canadians grew accustomed to rising incomes and living standards. We came to believe, as parents, that our children would lead lives more prosperous than ours. We came to believe, as wage-earners, that our economy would continue to expand and our incomes would continue to grow. We came to believe, as citizens, that the most pressing of our social ills could be alleviated. We came to believe, as possessors of a blessed land with seemingly limitless natural resources, that our lives could be infinitely enriched, our fortunes infinitely multiplied.

In the nineties, we have come to believe that these assumptions were wrong, that as individuals, and as a society, we have been living beyond our means, on borrowed time, borrowed money, and finite resources. We have also come to see that the technological revolution that is transforming the workplace in every industrial society is only making matters worse. That millions of unemployed and underemployed Canadians must continue to endure short-term pain to guarantee Canada's long-term gain in the burgeoning global economy has become an article of faith in corporate boardrooms and political backrooms. Before we, the citizenry, embrace the faith fully, however, we would do well to ask ourselves whether it is the only possible scenario in the circumstances, and to ponder what scenario would be better.

Although techno-confusion is rampant in the nineties, the technological "revolution" that is "creating" such havoc and anxiety in the workplace is by no means a new phenomenon. Technological change has been ongoing in every industrialized society. Similarly, the beginnings of what economists call "structural unemployment" date back to, and flow from, Canada's great leap into the industrial age. The availability of cheap electricity and the widespread adoption of organizational efficiencies in the workplace sparked Canada's emergence as an industrial nation; they also made it possible, for the first time, for manufacturers to increase their production while reducing their workforces. Even as they created more jobs, they created the potential for widespread unemployment whenever production outstripped demand.

The potential for a destructive shift in the ratio of output to labour—the definition of structural unemployment—was masked by the rapid growth of new industries during the first three decades of the century, but was a primary cause of the Great Depression. The Second World War favourably changed the ratio in the forties, as urgent demands for labour and goods drew thousands of women into the workforce, and provided abundant employment for young and old alike.

During the postwar years, Canadians, abrim with confidence and optimism, rushed to buy the flood of consumer goods made possible—and affordable—by the new technologies, processes, and materials developed for the war effort. Instead of making guns and bombs, manufacturers were turning out the weapons of the good life—televisions, hi-fi sets and transistor radios, refrigerators, washing machines and freezers, automobiles, and split-level bungalows—providing employment for everyone who wished to work.

The fifties and sixties have been called the Golden Age of capitalism, the charmed years when the Western economic system seemed poised to deliver it all: rising incomes, not just for the middle classes, but for everyone; employment, not just for the highly skilled, but for all who were able and willing to work; income security, not just for the well-to-do, but for all those unable to provide it for themselves. Productivity was high, inflation was low, jobs were plentiful.

In the late sixties, however, a dark cloud appeared on the horizon. In the midst of prosperity, the seeds of inflation had been sown. Soon, the growing concentration of corporate power, a largely unregulated market, and the rapid growth of foreign ownership of the Canadian economy would push up the inflation rate. By the end of the decade, control of 60 per cent of Canadian manufacturing and 90 per cent of such industries as petroleum and rubber were in foreign hands. Large multinational corporations had begun to bypass tariff restrictions by building and operating branch plants in many countries, including Canada.

As the inflation rate crept up, the economy cooled. Although few people noticed it, the structural unemployment that extraordinary circumstances had held in abeyance since the Great Depression began to dog the Canadian economy again. Around the time of the country's jubilant centennial celebrations in 1967, real wages in Canada stopped growing. By the early eighties, although inflation concealed the trend, they began to decline.

The explanations for the turn-around were complex, but

they reflected two broad trends. First, higher-paying manufacturing jobs were being replaced by lower-paying jobs
in the service sector. Like "technology" today, "automation"
was seen then as a serious threat to the livelihoods of thousands of Canadians. Second, fierce competition from Japan,
Western Europe, and East Asia was forcing Canadian wages
down. Imported goods, often of superior quality or cachet
to home-made products, claimed consumers' loyalties.
Manufacturers were moving their operations offshore, or
were threatening to do so, in search of cheaper labour and
lower overheads. Production in Canada began to exceed
demand.

Inevitably, unemployment rose, both in absolute numbers and as a percentage of the total labour force; and the
postwar assumption of full employment and ever-
expanding economic growth was called into question. Low-
skill jobs paying $10 to $15 an hour began to be replaced, if
at all, by jobs with much lower wages. For the first time,
jobs in "service" industries outnumbered those in manufacturing. Some jobs disappeared altogether, as automation
made them superfluous. This was structural unemployment, an unexpected and costly turn of events. This time,
however, Canada was much better prepared than it had
been during the Great Depression to cushion the blow.

Industrialized urban societies have always struggled with
the problem of what to do with the unemployed in poor
economic times. Traditionally their plight has translated
into rising costs and declining revenues for the state, and
their joblessness has created the potential for social unrest.
The cruel equations of "poor" with "unemployed," and
"social assistance" with moral reprehensibility and criminality, had a long, sad history in pre-war Canada; yet even
before the economic prosperity of the postwar years
encouraged well-off Canadians to look more benignly upon
their less fortunate neighbours, the country had made
progress in solving them.

The first compulsory national unemployment-insurance

program—funded jointly by employers, employees, and the federal government in response to an unemployment rate that rose to 20 per cent during the Great Depression—was established in 1940, and a family-allowance program was introduced a year later. Together, they addressed the most pressing needs of the jobless, and ushered in a compassionate new philosophy: that in prosperous modern societies dependent upon an educated and healthy workforce, the provision of relief in times of high unemployment is, like health care and education, a shared responsibility.

Acting on this philosophy, Canadians, still mindful of the human miseries of the Depression years, adopted bold new measures in the fifties and sixties to guard against inequities in access to health care, and to ensure that no Canadian, young or old, would lack the basic necessities of life. The universal Old Age Security program was instituted in 1951; a universal health plan and the Canada Pension Plan arrived in the mid-sixties. Most Canadians were rightly proud that these programs existed and agreed that they were just, prudent, and economically sound.

During the seventies, Canada drifted into "stagflation," an unprecedented coincidence of high inflation, high unemployment, and sustained slow-down in the growth rates of production. At about the same time, changes in the country's tax structure shifted more of the tax burden that sustained the country's social programs onto middle- and lower-income earners, and away from corporations and the wealthiest Canadians.

Stagflation baffled economists, who were accustomed to thinking of unemployment and inflation as two seats on a see-saw: If one went up, the other had invariably gone down. In response to this unusual economic configuration, the Liberal government in Ottawa restricted the money supply, a "monetarist" intervention that further slowed economic growth and gave Canadians a preview of the kind of rigorous "tight-money" approach to managing the economy that would become so familiar to them a decade later.

The trends towards chronic unemployment and declining real incomes became especially apparent when the economy plunged into recession in 1981. The debate on what corrective measures should be taken to counter them unfolded predictably. Voices on the political left argued that an appropriate response was to expand government's role in job creation, expand government's investment in technology and infrastructure, and expand government's investment in education to order make Canada more competitive. Voices on the right argued that what was needed was much greater reliance on the private sector and the free market to further Canada's position in the world, and thereby solve its employment problems at home. Canadian corporations would become more competitive abroad and more productive at home, they said, if governments would just get off their backs.

In 1984, with the country emerging from the recession, Paul Hellyer, the veteran Toronto Liberal who served as a cabinet minister in the governments of Louis St. Laurent, Lester Pearson, and Pierre Trudeau, offered a less conventional view of what had gone wrong with Canada's economy. His book *Jobs for All: Capitalism on Trial* took up the Canadian Conference of Catholic Bishops' bitter condemnation of government policies that countenanced high unemployment. (These had been described as "demonic" in their 1983 manifesto, *Ethical Reflections of the Economic Crisis.*) Hellyer's book was a spirited attack on the neoconservatism of British prime minister Margaret Thatcher and U.S. president Ronald Reagan, and on what Hellyer called their "sadistic" monetaristic policies.

The years of inflation since the early seventies and the policies employed to regulate Western economies "had wreaked havoc around the world," Hellyer wrote. "Millions of people lost their jobs, some lost their homes and, worst of all, many lost their dreams of a better life for themselves and their children." Then he posed the big question: "Why," he asked, "has the economic system that gave us the 'golden' decades of the '50s and '60s now come to an apparent impasse, where runaway inflation or massive unemployment seem the only alternatives? Could there be a structural flaw in the capitalist system?"

The urgency informing those questions subsided soon after, as Canada, now governed by the Mulroney Tories, recovered from the recession. Unemployment rates fell, interest rates stabilized, inflation rates declined, life went on—for many Canadians more prosperously than before. A trend towards corporate expansion and diversification, in which large corporations acquired smaller companies whose products had little or nothing to do with their own, reflected a mood of high optimism.

Hellyer's book, and the warnings of like-minded observers who questioned the wisdom of stringent monetarist solutions, were largely forgotten. But they presaged a debate that is erupting in the mid-nineties. In the midst of a debt and deficit "crisis" that has somehow become the monolithic context for every discussion of social and economic policy in this decade, questions about capitalism's "fatal flaw" are coming back to haunt us. The issues of corporate morality raised by Paul Hellyer and the Conference of Catholic Bishops are surfacing again. *Should* the right to gainful employment be as fundamental as freedom of speech? *Has* Canada's economic system come to an impasse? *Are* runaway inflation and massive unemployment the only alternatives? *Can* the free market solve our problems, as the Thatcherites, Reaganites, Mulroneyites, and now the Chrétien Liberals insist it can? *Is* there a fatal structural flaw in the capitalist system?

It is no accident that these questions are being asked now, in the aftermath of the worst economic downturn since the Great Depression, when more Canadians have a direct and immediate stake in the answers than ever before. The recession of the early eighties was severe—the unemployment rate reached 13.5 per cent in August 1983—but Canada's recovery was reassuring. Moreover, because high inflation effectively redistributes income from low earners on fixed incomes to high earners with such fixed obligations as long-term mortgages, many financially comfortable Canadians profited greatly from the economic factors that caused the recession, while many others weathered the downturn without great personal discomfort. The rich had become richer; working-class Canadians had taken it on the chin; and the middle classes had soldiered on, sympathetic but largely unscathed.

When another recession closed in on us in 1989, Canadians braced for a similar bad patch, and hoped that it would be brief; but the downturn dragged on, and on, and on in Canada, long after the U.S. economy had turned around. Many of us wondered if this might be, in part at least, a "made-at-home" recession—not, as most economists insisted, the inevitable result of a worldwide economic malaise. Then, when economic indicators began to rally, we began to wonder why our job market was failing to rally, as it always had after earlier recessions in Canada, and as it had in the United States after this one. Finally, with unprecedented numbers of Canadians losing their jobs long after the recession was officially "over," the middle classes, most of whom—with the noteworthy exception of small-business owners—had weathered the "official" recession with little personal discomfort, began to grow alarmed.

Much of their anxiety focused on the security of their own jobs, a new worry for most financially comfortable, well-educated Canadians under age sixty. The aftermath of this recession was puzzling to them: Suddenly their employers were in a mad dash to flatten, de-layer, and downsize their organizations. Suddenly, they could make do not only with fewer workers, but also with fewer managers. For middle-class Canadians, the possibility that *their* jobs might now be at risk was a novel and disturbing development.

The anxiety trigger for many people was the realization that new technologies could actually replace *them*, a sobering thought for those who had never had to concern themselves with technology in their working lives. A decade ago, people joked that computers were forcing men to learn to type. Then it dawned on all of us that if we couldn't use a word processor or manipulate a spreadsheet or electronically access information, our jobs were at risk. Worse, they might be at risk even if we could.

Middle-class job fears were compounded by a series of related psychological shocks. Significant among them was Canadians' growing realization that their savings might not be sufficient to maintain their lifestyles in retirement, especially if they were forced or enticed into retiring early. The imminent demise of Old Age Security for the financially comfortable was a small blow. The de-inflation of house prices was a greater shock. Most home-owners in Canada have enjoyed ever-rising real-estate prices. Until recently, once the mortgage was discharged, a home was at least as bankable as a well-managed retirement plan. When the bottom suddenly dropped out of the housing market in the late eighties, many recent home-buyers found that they owed more on their mortgages than their houses were worth. Those who had been whittling away at mortgages for years discovered that they no longer had a nest egg but an asset of deflated value.

These painful developments must be put into perspective. Blue-collar workers have always had to deal with the prospect of lay-offs in economic downturns, just as they have always had to deal with the knowledge that their jobs might disappear permanently when new technology comes on-line. They have also known that at some time in their lives, they might have to rely on state-provided assistance, in the form of unemployment insurance or welfare, until the next job materialized.

In the nineties these prospects confront a much larger percentage of the population, at the very time when the safety net is unravelling, and at the very time when we have lost confidence in the economy's capacity to generate good new jobs. As the federal government and the provinces have vigorously attacked their deficits, the structural underpinnings that have long protected Canada's middle class—and, indeed, that have enabled Canada to sustain such a large middle class—are disappearing. Moreover, job losses, especially for people age forty-five and over, are likely to be permanent. Many Canadians who expected to work until they were sixty-five now don't expect to work again, at least not in jobs remotely equivalent to the ones they have lost. For them, unemployment means a long-term drop in earnings and even less for their retirement.

Could it be, Canadians are wondering, that we are destined to be nothing more than the helpless victims of a global upheaval every bit as cataclysmic as the Industrial Revolution was to nineteenth-century Europe? Or do we have choices available to us, actions that we might take to regain our equilibrium? To some observers, it seems that we do not. The cataclysmic scenario has been argued with considerable vigour by workplace pessimists. The U.S. economist Jeremy Rifkin, an insightful and influential commentator on economic trends, premises his entire analysis of workplace change and global employment on the eventual disappearance of work.

"The Information Age has arrived," Rifkin wrote in his 1995 bestseller, *The End of Work*. "After years of wishful forecasts and false starts, new computer and communication technologies are finally making their long-anticipated impact on the workplace and the economy, throwing the world community into the grip of a third great industrial revolution." In the years ahead, Rifkin predicts, "new, more sophisticated software technologies are going to bring civilization ever closer to a near-workerless world."

Rifkin has little to say about Canada's problems, or about Canada's unique economic ties to and dependence upon the U.S. economy; but his analyses of the emerging global economy cannot be reassuring for Canadians. It has been fashionable for technology optimists to argue that the big losers in the new economy will be the low-skill workers who have always been vulnerable in bad economic times, and to insist that middle-class, white-collar workers in the information- and financial-services industries will emerge as winners. This may be so, but it is not likely to solve our problems.

"In the past," Rifkin points out, "when a technological revolution threatened the wholesale loss of jobs in an economic sector, a new sector emerged to absorb the surplus labor." This time, he says, it's not going to happen, because "the only new sector on the horizon is the knowledge sector, an elite group of industries and professional disciplines responsible for ushering in the new high-tech automated economy of the future." While the knowledge sector will grow steadily, Rifkin cautions, it will remain small compared with the number of people displaced by technology.

Even if Canada succeeds in rising to the challenges of the "knowledge revolution" by restructuring our workplaces, refocusing our school and university curricula to meet corporate needs, and concentrating our energies and financial resources on competing in the global arena, as the most extreme free-market enthusiasts would have us do, difficulties will still confront us. One of these difficulties is that the "knowledge" industries—financial services, management, media, entertainment, information services— may prove to be the most vulnerable to global competition and job-killing technological change. When money and information can move around the world electronically in a split second, it matters very little where corporate headquarters or workers are. Giant, globe-girdling multinationals' concern for the well-being of the local economies in which they operate is hardly a top priority.

This troubling aspect of global competition compromises the loyalties of many home-grown corporations who have built their reputations—sometimes justifiably, sometimes not—on being good Canadian citizens, but who now wish to compete in the global arena. It also creates difficulties for us—as employees, as consumers, as taxpayers, and as citizens. Canadian banks, to take an obvious example, have long traded on the contributions they have made to nation building and the role they have played in the continuing economic strength of the country. They have also stressed their abiding loyalty to us, their customers. Now, however, the banks are focusing on their prospects in the global arena, where, like the miller, they assure us they will find straw to be spun into gold. In preparation for their global forays, they are diversifying, restructuring their operations, introducing new technologies, and seeking ways to become even more profitable at home.

These competitive initiatives, in so far as they kill jobs, penalize small, local businesses, and extract money from our pockets to cover proliferating service charges, would seem to call their loyalty to us into question. From the industry's point of view, however, these unpleasant-nesses—along with the considerable competitive advantages banks enjoy by virtue of their quasi-public status—are simply the prices we must pay to enable them to compete aggressively in the wider world. As Helen Sinclair, the outgoing president of the Canadian Bankers Association, cautioned in April 1996, any government decision to tax the banks more would mean that "by definition, we will not play in the world leagues.... At present, no Canadian bank makes the grade globally on the basis of its size. And we're slipping."

The bankers have a case. They are likely correct when they tell us that—large, privileged, and powerful as they are at home—they are not large, privileged, and powerful *enough* to thrive in the global economy. They also have an expectation: that as they sally forth to compete in the world, Ottawa, by turning a blind eye to their oligopolistic, anti-competitive practices at home, will continue to protect their interests—and profits—in an effort to help them achieve their global ambitions.

Canadian banks have a shot at success in the global economy. It will, however, be an uphill battle. In the United

States, a decade of bank mega-mergers has created ever-larger, ever-more-powerful global competitors. Japanese and Swiss banks, too, are consolidating into the largest banks in the world. Competition from these mammoth institutions will put great pressure on Canadian banks to become ever leaner at our expense. Our bankers, to meet the competition, will continue to press for preferential treatment from Ottawa, as they will continue to tailor their own operations to make them more competitive.

In the meantime, Canadians are already paying a steep price for the measures the banks and many other global warriors are taking to transform their enterprises into global powerhouses. In their blind rush to ready themselves for the future, they have downsized, restructured, and re-engineered us into a corner, creating an atmosphere of fear that has caused many Canadians to lose hope—and to abandon as unrealistic and misguided many of the values we once shared. For the first time in more than half a century, significant numbers of Canadians are blaming the poor for their poverty, and the jobless for their lack of work. For the first time in more than half a century, significant numbers of us, including many of our politicians, are blaming the victims for the crime.

It is dreaming to think that every Canadian corporation can withstand fierce global competition, just as it is dreaming to think that those corporations that do fare well in the global marketplace will generate enough jobs to solve Canada's unemployment problems. Like other multinationals, they will take their jobs elsewhere, and—short of deliberately transforming Canada into a third-world country with third-world wages—there is little we can do to prevent it.

Or is there? Many thoughtful observers of the emerging global economy, as we shall see throughout this book, say that there are steps we can take—that, indeed, we *must* take—to protect ourselves and our local economies from the devastations of technological change and globalization.

A careful examination of the fundamental assumptions underlying the neoconservative economic policies that have driven government decision making in most industrialized countries for the past twenty years, they say, will show that there are alternative courses of action to be considered, other measures we can take to mitigate the damage, different approaches we can adopt to address social dislocation and high unemployment, capitalism's "fatal flaws."

In Canada, that examination must begin with a critique of the twin neoconservative orthodoxies: that government has little legitimate role to play in moderating the excesses of the marketplace; and that government spending on social programs is the cause of our economic woes, including unemployment. Our obsession with high government deficits in the nineties has been driven by insistence that we cannot afford the social programs we have created over the last forty years. Our rising debt levels—and our dependence on foreign lenders to service them—became unsustainable, the argument goes, and our social programs were to blame. We have had no choice but to put things right, whatever the human cost.

Although no objective economist would agree that Canada's social programs were the sole cause of out-of-control deficits—and many would argue that they were not the cause at all—clearly there was truth in the argument that deficits in Ottawa and in many provinces had risen to unsustainable levels. Throughout the nineties, therefore, our governments took stringent measures to drive the deficits down. Now, from a fiscal point of view, it is equally clear that the deficit-reduction remedies they adopted have been highly effective.

The federal deficit is now under control, and most provinces are operating with balanced budgets or surpluses. The Paris-based Organization for Economic Co-operation and Development predicts that in 1997 Canada's budget deficit will fall well below 2 per cent of gross national product—for the second year in a row the smallest GNP deficit among the G-7 countries, and well below the European Union's average of 4.9 per cent. Moreover, the 1996 report of the World Economic Forum on global competitiveness lists Canada in eighth place among forty-nine countries.

The Bank of Canada, in its all-consuming effort to wrestle down the deficits, has accepted the neoconservative orthodoxy that high unemployment is the price we must pay for these successes, that economies cannot expand much faster than 2 per cent annually without triggering inflation. Now, however, growing numbers of critics of its relentless low-inflation policy are reminding us that the point of free-trade agreements and the thrust of globalization have been towards a radically different kind of economy, in which the old economic orthodoxies no longer apply. They are also warning that the monetarist policies of the central bankers have become counter-productive.

It is time, they say, to abandon the received wisdom that low interest rates and low unemployment inevitably translate into high inflation. Instead, they say, modern economies need low-interest policies that create, not kill, jobs. The respected Massachusetts Institute of Technology economist Lester Thurow, for one, has long argued that the obsession with pushing inflation rates down not only ensures that economies continually teeter on the brink of recession, but also guarantees that when they do slide into recession, they will take much longer to recover.

Thurow's is a voice from the left; but increasingly it is not only the long-time ideological opponents of strict monetarism who are questioning the wisdom of the road taken by low-inflation zealots. Observers across the political spectrum are raising doubts about the wisdom of policies that tolerate brutally high unemployment. Ethan Kapstein, director of studies at the conservative New York–based Council of Foreign Relations, expressed his reservations in the journal *Foreign Affairs* in April 1996. Western countries, Kapstein says, *must* generate more jobs to help those who have lost out in the rush to globalization, if only to prevent a return to protectionism and damaging trade wars. The low-inflation policies that have killed jobs, he adds, have come at the worst possible time. "Just when working people need the nation state as a buffer from the world economy," he points out, "it is abandoning them."

Some Canadian economists, such as the best-selling author Nuala Beck, blame Canada's woes on U.S. policy makers and our vulnerability to their inflation-fighting strategies. "You would never know it from the daily newspapers, or from that cranky crowd at the U.S. Federal Reserve Board, who raise our interest rates for no good reason," she observed in her 1995 book, *Excelerate*. "They still accord the venerable industries of the old economy a center-stage significance that is no longer warranted by their size." The "old economy," Beck points out, now accounts for only about 13 per cent of Canada's gross domestic product, and "after more than a decade of downsizing, many of these old-economy industries are rather small ... yet the people running out-of-date institutions still base their economic assumptions, and *our* interest rates," on their performance and behaviour.

Others, however, have become sceptical of arguments that Canada must continue to march to the U.S. drumbeat. William Thorsell, editor of *The Globe and Mail*—the most influential of media apologists for the neoconservative agenda set by the Mulroney government—expressed impatience with the low-inflation policies of the central bankers in an April 1996 column. Discussing a "passionate" appeal for lower interest rates to create stronger economic growth by Felix Rohatyn—"the Wall Street investment banker who declined U.S. president Bill Clinton's invitation to serve as deputy chairman of the Federal Reserve when purse-lipped neo-con Republicans made it clear they would veto him"—Thorsell lashed out at the "timid" Bank of Canada for its zero-inflation policy. "The Republicans and U.S. Fed are too timid for Mr. Rohatyn," he declared. "The Liberals and the Bank of Canada are too timid for me."

Even the conservative, Toronto-based C.D. Howe Institute, although it continued to defend a vigorous low-inflation policy, complained that the Bank of Canada has routinely pushed its strategy too far. "The tactics of monetary policy in the early 1990s have hurt growth and job creation," an institute study released in April 1996 noted, adding that the Bank has a habit of responding to weakness in the Canadian dollar by raising short-term interest rates too much. "Each time the Bank has restricted the money supply in recent years," the report observed, "inflation has fallen well below its own inflation-control targets." "The problem," the study held, "is not that the Bank of Canada adopted a tight-money policy in order to meet its inflation targets, but that its policy has actually been tighter than those targets required."

That the C.D. Howe Institute, one of the instigators of, and most vocal cheerleaders for, a strict low-inflation monetary policy, should be softening its views on these matters is noteworthy because, for more than a decade, anyone who has suggested that the goal of non-inflationary growth is attainable has been chastised by monetarist economists and shouted down by deficit-busters such as Michael Walker of Vancouver's conservative, business-financed Fraser Institute. Walker is still shouting, trying to bully Canadians into maintaining our deficit-obsessed mind-set.

As the human consequences of their remedies become clearer, however, many Canadians who endorsed them by voting for Reform federally, or for the ultra-conservative governments of Mike Harris in Ontario and Ralph Klein in Alberta, are rejecting their arguments. As a result, the debate over jobs and joblessness is shifting fast. Although Canadians were once content to blame government overspending on social programs for everything that has gone wrong with Canada's economy—including high unemployment—there is a growing realization that there are other factors to consider and other forces at work—and that the advocates of continuing the war on the deficit may be acting out of sheer corporate self-interest.

The organizations that are most outspoken about deficit reduction—the Canadian Bankers Association, the National Council on Business Issues, the National Citizens' Coalition, the Fraser Institute, the C.D. Howe Institute, among many others—have always been virulent opponents of government intervention in the market. For them, the nineties have been heady and agreeable times. Rising deficits have been a gift from on high, enabling them to press their agendas more relentlessly, with little opposition from Canadians.

As the debate shifts, however, their increasingly strident and sanctimonious rhetoric is wearing thin and their dogged efforts to hold the high ground are growing tiresome. Few Canadians would disagree that we have learned a painful lesson in the last few years: that we must pay for what we receive from government. But many of us also believe that it is possible for our governments to be fiscally prudent and socially responsible at the same time, and that now—when we are once again in a position to do so—we should be seeking fresh policies that will mend our tattered social programs, heal our divided society, and put Canadians back to work.

Why, then, do conservative politicians and corporate leaders and their lobby groups continue to advocate the adoption of even more stringent deficit-fighting measures? Could it be that there is more to the deficit-slashing mania of the nineties than meets the eye? Could it be that under cover of the deficits, the noisy proponents of privatization, zero inflation, and free-market solutions to every economic and social problem we face are leading us astray? Could it be that Canada's dismal employment picture is a flaw of our own devising?

Could it be that the King has been deceived? Could it be that it is time to ask whether the miller and his emboldened band of Rumpelstiltskins care a fig for the people of the kingdom?

Chapter 2
Globalization and Globaloney: The Gospel of Workplace Change

"If your daughter is truly as clever as you say she is, bring her to my palace tomorrow so that I may try her unusual talent," said the King to the miller.

Let us, for a moment, consider the miller. Perhaps he was a common man, seeking an audience with the King to ask for relief from the taxes levied upon his mill or the resolution of a dispute with his neighbour over a debt unpaid, a tool borrowed and not returned, a river dammed, a horse stolen.

Perhaps he was mad, and truly believed that his daughter could spin straw into gold. Perhaps he was a cunning man, scheming to trick the King into marrying his daughter. Or perhaps he was a clever, ambitious, aggrieved man, who had suffered financial set-backs because he had been prevented from selling straw to the gullible on the promise that it was worth its weight in gold.

Let us say that this miller was a clever man, a shrewd man with a deep grievance. Let us say also that he sought favours from the King: an easing of the rules that regulated his business practices *and the operations of his mill, or a break on his taxes.*

Let us say that the miller wished to create a demand in the kingdom for straw, not because he truly believed that his daughter knew how to spin straw into gold, but because he himself wished to profit from its sale.

Let us imagine further that the miller knew of the kingdom's great debts and the King's troubled state of mind, and believed that he could persuade him that his beneficence had been misplaced, his compassion misguided. Perhaps he believed he could persuade the King that there were measures he could take—involving the purchase of straw—to discharge his debts and bring prosperity to his kingdom.

Perhaps he believed he could even persuade the King that his daughter knew how to spin the straw into gold.

Imagine that!

Economists speak of high labour costs "pricing people out of work," of structural unemployment "displacing workers," of "increasing the productivity" of the workforce. Traditionally, corporate leaders translated these phrases into less threatening, more impersonal terms. They spoke of the need for "flexibility," or "responsiveness," or "competitive repositioning," vague concepts that made no reference to the people whose lives would be affected by the changes they wished to bring about. The rhetoric of workplace change in the nineties, however, lacks even these civilities, deriving, as most of it does, from the world of new technologies.

The words in play in many corporate boardrooms are cold, hard, mechanical. Companies have been "re-engineered," as though they were pieces of machinery. Workforces have been "downsized" or "right-sized," as though they were computer-generated models. Workers, like the inanimate objects they manufacture, may be "reorganized," "redirected," or "reoriented" at will. Corporate hierarchies have been "restructured," "flattened," "de-layered." Workers have been "de-hired," "de-selected," "severed." Entire industries have been "de-jobbed."

What is missing from the images these words conjure, of course, is living, breathing human beings. Increasingly, as journalists and commentators have used this jargon to explain the global unemployment crisis and the dawning of the "information age" to the rest of us, the language of the corporate world, coined by "management experts," has crept into our everyday parlance, as though these words— and therefore the assumptions behind them—were the only ones available to describe the changes going on around us. As a result, we have come to see our changing workplaces from the point of view of those initiating the changes: as venues that *must* be re-engineered if they are to meet the challenges of the future.

Although they may be new to us, however, many of the words and theories that seem to offer fresh insights into the workplace of the nineties are not new at all. For example, Peter Drucker, the prolific U.S. theorist usually credited with founding the discipline of management studies, coined the terms "knowledge work" and "knowledge worker" nearly forty years ago, and has been writing about how "information technology" changes organizations and jobs ever since. In the late sixties, in *The Age of Discontinuity*, Drucker pointed out that despite the phenomenal economic progress made since the Second World War, the structure of the economy and its leading corporations had changed relatively little in fifty years. Old technologies, he said, were "played out," and "radical restructuring" would be needed in order "to exploit" new ones.

Drucker did not, however, speak of these changes as they are spoken of today. Writing about the role of government in the workplace "turbulence" he anticipated, Drucker observed that "what is needed is a clear, open, and firm commitment to the livelihood, productive employment, and placement of people ... a commitment to anticipating redundancies, to retraining people, and to placing them." It is "not a matter of money," he cautioned. Rather, "it is primarily a matter of vision and of leadership. Without it, the economies of the developed countries will not be able to adapt to the changes of tomorrow. The economic opportunities will instead become monstrous threats to them."

In Canada, as in most Western economies, adapting to these changes *has*, of course, become almost entirely a matter of money. Our vision has been tightly constrained by high levels of indebtedness to foreign lenders, and by our governments' obsession with their deficits, an obsession carefully nurtured by corporate interests whose underlying goal is to diminish the role of government in the Canadian economy so that they may get on with their global dreams, regardless of how many dreams they dash at home.

In the eighties, the Mulroney Tories made much of their commitment to economic policies that would create better lives for Canadians. They promised us "Jobs, Jobs, Jobs" in two election campaigns, even as the deficit grew and dependence on offshore lenders increased. Jobs, jobs, jobs were also a central 1993 election promise of the Chrétien Liberals, who ridiculed then prime minister Kim Campbell when she was forthright—some would say foolish— enough to admit during the campaign that the unemployment rate in Canada was not likely to fall much below 10 per cent before the turn of the century. Under the Liberals, the private and public sector "de-jobbing" has continued apace, as both Tories and Liberals knew it would, given the stringent deficit-cutting policies to which both parties were, and are, so deeply committed.

It is not my intention to in rehearse detail the ideological battles over free trade and deficit and debt reduction that have preoccupied some Canadians in the nineties, although it will be necessary to address these disputes from time to time in later chapters. For now, let us simply accept assurances from federal Finance minister Paul Martin that we are through the worst of it, that the Canadian economy is on the mend, that the job market is picking up, fervently hoping that he is right.

It *is* my intention, however, to examine why so many of our corporate leaders reject such assurances out of hand. Why do they adamantly refuse to identify any point, above zero deficits at every level of government, as one at which we can declare that enough debt and deficit reduction has been accomplished to justify new approaches to managing the Canadian economy? Why do they continue to insist that the cuts must go still deeper, that interest rates must stay up to drive inflation to zero, that the human devastation of high unemployment must continue?

Could it be that they have more to gain from prolonging this painful process than from endorsing new policies that have a chance of restoring an economy that actually creates jobs? Do they realize that the harsh measures they advocate could come back to haunt them, and all Canadians?

Take, as one example among many, the corporate determination to excise ruthlessly the middle layers of their own managerial ranks, and their insistence that all governments must do likewise. Targeting the jobs and ridiculing the usefulness of those who once enjoyed a measure of respect— and a measure of security—not only undermines managers' confidence, but also destabilizes entire workplaces, undermining confidence more generally. This, in turn, contributes to high levels of societal anxiety, inhibiting the consumer spending required to spark job creation. Can these outcomes be in anyone's interest, including their own?

Ironically, Peter Drucker was among the earliest and most vocal management experts to target middle managers as expendable in the knowledge economy. He insisted that in traditional organizations, most "managers" do not actually manage. He may also have been responsible, unwittingly, for the low repute in which the managerial classes are currently held by so many of their employers. "They relay orders downward and information upward," Drucker wrote in his 1993 book, *Post-Capitalist Society*, and "when information becomes available, they become redundant."

This pronouncement resonated with large employers, many of whom, having eliminated the jobs of as many rank-and-file employees as their businesses could tolerate, began to eliminate more senior, more highly paid positions in their organizations. Sustained by advice such as Drucker's that in knowledge-based companies, superiors cannot possibly know anything about the jobs of their subordinates because they have never held them, corporate downsizers, looking to flatten their managerial hierarchies, mowed down legions of middle managers, many of whom will never work again.

Having revamped their own organizations, many of these same corporate leaders insistently urged public-sector employers to do the same. Most governments in Canada are now taking their advice, implicitly accepting the questionable proposition that governments ought to be run like corporations, and therefore must be radically downsized too. Ironically, however, as governments slash away at jobs, many private-sector employers are wondering whether they might have been too hasty, and too harsh, in their downsizing exercises. Peter Drucker's disdain for middle managers grew from his benign and optimistic conviction that information would "empower" employees, transforming them into independent thinkers and self-starters who no longer needed to be "managed." But the typical downsized workplace of the nineties in Canada is not a place that empowers most of those who toil there.

When people are confident about their jobs and their futures, they are free to take charge of their work, to be creative, to question entrenched practices and policies, to improve the work that they do. When they are besieged and frightened, they keep their heads down and their creative thoughts to themselves. They shun new ideas, trying not to do or say anything that might be construed as criticism of corporate practices and policies. Instead of opening channels of creative communication within an organization, the elimination of middle managers, it would seem, plugs them up, or dismantles them.

Similarly, the introduction of such new technologies as voice mail to effect savings and efficiencies can instead build barriers that stifle creativity. Their availability and convenience may encourage employers to adopt tools that require no human interaction at all, forgetting that creativity thrives in company. There is no shortage of such systems on the market. A Cleveland company, TelServe Inc., for example, has devised an automated, interactive telephone service that interviews job applicants who are willing to call a 1-800 number and to answer a series of detailed, prerecorded questions about their professional qualifications and their personal lives.

In addition to obvious concerns about privacy, the system raises interesting questions about the motivations of an organization that would want to use it. Why would a company want to banish all human contact in the initial stages of the hiring process? Several answers come to mind. First, such a system would obviously be a timesaver for overworked human-resource departments, who could use it to screen the first round of applicants, and therefore effect a savings for the company. Second, it could eliminate the unpleasant task of telling applicants they have been rejected out of hand.

But consider the TelServe system from the applicant's point of view. No chance to ask questions about the job, or about the company. No opportunity to seek clarification of the questions asked. No way to demonstrate a quick mind or a winning personality. No need for potential employers to tell applicants why they are unsuitable. More ominously, no need for employers to tell applicants anything at all—including whether they might have been rejected for reasons that have nothing to do with their qualifications: their accents, for example. Might not an employer wishing to bypass equal-opportunity legislation be able to use such a system to screen for race, gender, or ethnicity?

Contrast the impersonality of such technologies with the advice routinely dispensed to job seekers on how to find employment in the nineties. "Anticipate what the employer will ask." "Learn as much as you can about the company before you go to the interview." "Be prepared to discuss the job you are seeking knowledgeably." "Ask questions about the position." "Ask questions about the company." "Look your interviewer in the eye." "Sell yourself." In effect, any parity in the relationship between employer and prospective employee has been destroyed. The applicant has become a supplicant. The employer has become an inscrutable, arbitrary, all-powerful god.

The employer has also become a coward. Cowardice is endemic in the harsh economic climate of the nineties. When organizations downsize radically, as the Ontario civil service did in the spring of 1996, those responsible for deciding who will get the chop often leave underlings to carry out the execution. One senior manager in Toronto, faced with the task of releasing a valued employee with a new baby, a new mortgage, and a husband getting the chop in another department the same morning, made an appointment to have her hair coloured to avoid having to deliver the news herself.

Still, it is not hard to empathize with the cowardly manager. She was distressed by a situation over which she had no control, other than to decide whom to fire. Across Canada, human-resources departments are discovering that the job they were hired to do—to look after the interests of employees—is not the job they are doing. Instead, they are being asked to engage in activities that are manifestly not in employees' best interests—for example, to fire them. Is it any wonder, then, that downsizing leads to significant declines in managerial productivity and morale?

The phenomenon of "survivor sickness" is well documented. It is the malady suffered not only by those who have participated in the process of downsizing, but also by all those who remain at their posts after their colleagues have been laid off or dismissed. Its immediate symptoms are guilt, frustration, unease, and sadness. But survivor sickness has other, longer-term, effects as well. Employees who keep their jobs lose trust in their employers, come to resent them, feel betrayed by them. They seek reasons for what has happened and, not finding reasons that make sense, they lay blame.

In time, they realize that they are being asked to take up the slack, to work harder and longer for an employer who has not provided adequate reasons why this should be so, or adequate recompense the extra effort. Moreover, when their salaries are frozen or in decline, they have little reason to believe that they *should* be working harder, especially when corporate fortunes and executive compensation are on the rise.

The loss of faith is perhaps greatest among those who work for corporations that are simultaneously downsizing and reporting healthy profits, but it also afflicts those in the public sector, where profitability is not the issue. This loss of confidence is costly to everyone. The cost to the survivors may be measured in emotional and physical terms: anger, depression, fatigue. The cost to the employer may be measured in lost productivity, organizational chaos, and loss of respect and loyalty.

Many corporate employers decided in the last decade that these were acceptable, if disagreeable, prices to pay for honing their enterprises' competitive edge in the new economy. Many also discovered that parading their lay-off announcements before the public improved the price of their shares on international markets, justifying the havoc they were creating. Plant closings, lay-offs, wage roll-backs, and permanent job loss, they came to believe, were the unfortunate—but inevitable—consequences of their quest for enhanced profitability in a fast-changing world.

In a recent *Financial Post* supplement on management consultants, in an article by Louise Kinross entitled "Boom

Times Seen for Industry," Coopers & Lybrand senior partner Richard Hossack explained why the management-consulting industry is booming. "The public sector knows it's in trouble and has to make major changes," Hossack observed. "Private companies have already taken their hits, got their minds around the cost issues, and want help growing the top line." Corporate employers, he added, are "looking globally and know there's a market out there for them somewhere, so they're not as concerned if the local economy fails a bit."

It is, of course, this lack of concern for the "local economy" that is infuriating Canadians. When local economies "fail a bit," people lose their livelihoods. Why on earth aren't these corporate employers concerned? What is it about "globalization" that justifies immiseration at home? In their book *Global Dreams*, Richard J. Barnet and John Cavanagh point out that globalization is "*the* most fashionable word of the 1990s," one "so portentous and wonderfully patient as to puzzle Alice in Wonderland and thrill the Red Queen because it means precisely whatever the user says it means. Just as poets and songwriters celebrated the rise of modern nationalism, so in our day corporate managers, environmental prophets, business philosophers, rock stars and writers of advertising copy offer themselves as poet laureates of the global village."

However, "much of the breathless talk about globalization we hear all around us," they argue, "is what the late Clare Boothe Luce used to call globaloney." The global economic system, which "prizes the efficient production of goods more than the dignity of human beings," is fragile, they warn, "because it depends on growth fueled by the expansion of consumption," yet requires a "fierce drive to eliminate work and cut wages." This, they say, "is clearly not the way to bring the crowds to the shopping malls and car lots."

Could Barnet and Cavanagh be right when they argue that smaller businesses have been sold a bill of goods by giant corporations, "who are becoming the world empires of the twenty-first century"? Their "architects and managers," they say "understand that the balance of power in world politics has shifted in recent years from territorially-bound governments to companies that can roam the world with no regard for the local economies in which they operate." Do the architects and managers of many smaller enterprises realize that they may have little chance of survival in a world populated by rapacious giants?

Many, it seems, are not prepared to risk being left out. Yet, after nearly a decade of panicky slash and burn, it has become clear to some employers that focusing their energies exclusively on the global economy—and remaking their companies to meet the global "challenge"—may be a mug's game for all but the most agile of information-age innovators and the largest of multinational corporations. They are also discovering that the downsizing culture not only erodes the morale of survivors, but also causes subtle, and usually unanticipated, dislocations and direction shifts at the heart of corporate enterprise.

Wall Street Journal reporter Bernard Wysocki, Jr., has described the changes this way: "New-product ideas languish," he wrote in "The Danger of Stretching Too Far" in August 1995. "Risk-taking dwindles because the culture of cost-cutting emphasizes the certainties of cutting costs over the uncertainties—and expense—of trying something new." On a more subtle level, Wysocki says, excessive cost-cutting tends to strengthen the authority of financial and accounting departments, who come to see it as their mandate "to control expenses rather than to monitor and evaluate new opportunities and investments." Downsizing, he cautions, can stifle creativity and innovation at the highest levels, compromising the very qualities that made the enterprise successful.

Downsizing can also erase the institutional memory of a successful business. When most of the people who conceived a company's long-term goals, or developed its product line, or created its marketing strategies vanish, old mistakes will likely be repeated and new mistakes made. One such mistake, as senior executives of more than one leaner and meaner corporation have discovered to their chagrin, is that the wrong people are let go because the managers who knew whom to keep have themselves been fired. Others have found that those responsible for making such decisions endeavour, above all, to protect their own jobs, at the expense of less senior people and rational planning.

Similarly, when the people who have nurtured a company's corporate image leave, there is a danger that the image will disintegrate. This is a lesson even the largest global competitors have had to learn. American Express, for example, jettisoned its long-time ad agency, Ogilvie & Mather, in 1992 as part of a massive restructuring, ignoring a thirty-year association that, in delivering such highly effective campaigns as "Don't Leave Home Without It," had furthered the company's fortunes around the world.

In its place, AMEX hired the trendy Chiat/Day/Mojo agency. They set about creating a new image in television ads that featured giant American Express charge cards looming over such familiar, and magnificent, landscapes as the Alps, where they looked more like environmental eyesores than global status symbols. When consumers, confused by this sudden abandonment of an image crafted so carefully for so long, defected to Visa and MasterCard in droves, American Express swiftly returned to Ogilvie & Mather, having learned that the loss of institutional memory can be an institution-threatening mistake.

Companies whose downsizing exercises are so extensive that they receive widespread media coverage also risk tarnishing their corporate images. When AT&T chairman Robert Allen announced the elimination of forty thousand jobs at the giant U.S. company early in 1996, the sheer size of the exercise triggered a *Newsweek* cover story bluntly entitled "Corporate Killers," sparking, as we shall see later, a virulent outbreak of anti-corporate sentiment in the

United States. Although AT&T shares rose on news of the cuts—a common market response to downsizing—they soon fell dramatically as outraged investors reacted to the adverse publicity. In response, AT&T took out ads, signed by Allen, in newspapers across the United States, begging other corporations to hire its cast-off workers—"among the best trained anywhere." Then it changed strategies, announcing that the cut-backs might be less severe, which further enraged Americans when *The Wall Street Journal* reported that despite the announcement, its cut-back targets remained unchanged.

When unemployment is high and local economies are in the doldrums, consumers do not look kindly upon companies who are seen to be exacerbating an already dire situation. Instead, they come to feel that the corporate executives who decide to let so many people go simply do not care about the economies in which they operate, and are contemptuous of the consumers who have made their enterprises prosper in the past.

Ordinary Canadians are beginning to understand that many of the most stringent, job-killing corporate measures have been carried out to prepare "Canada" to compete in the global economy; they, too, are also wondering whether they have been sold the globaloney of the nineties. As a rhetorical device, "globalization" has allowed employers and governments alike to justify almost anything they believe will enable them to make their operations more profitable or more cost-effective in the short term.

Many of us, however, even if we still have faith in the long-term vision, are questioning whether the rhetoric is overblown and the cost to local economies too high. As people have lost their jobs, they have stopped spending their money locally. They have stopped building houses, eating out, going to concerts and theatres, buying clothes and furniture and appliances. In short, they have stopped doing many of the things that keep local economies—and national economies—afloat, preferring to save any extra cash they may have to guard against an uncertain future. As a Central Housing and Mortgage Corporation report released in June 1996 noted, many Canadians aren't buying houses, not because they're broke, but because they're scared.

In the new economy, the argument goes, none of these things matters in the long run. So long as corporate strategists believe that they are preparing themselves for a more profitable future in the wider world, they are willing, as Richard Hossack pointed out, to dismiss the economic problems in their own backyards as unfortunate, but irrelevant. After all, they have reduced their complements, trimmed their payrolls, and taken control of their costs precisely in order to ensure that they can withstand a languishing economy at home.

But are their arguments valid? Several studies have shown that the leaders of many downsized companies are dissatisfied with the results. As long ago as 1993, an American Management Association survey, for example, found that fewer than half the several hundred downsized U.S. companies polled reported any increase in operating profits—and that many suffered a drop in profits after they reduced their workforces.

That many corporate employers are now changing their tune on downsizing in favour of a renewed emphasis on generating profit through growth in productivity—rather than creating cost-efficiencies by axing their workforces—is particularly galling. In depressing local economies by eliminating so many jobs, they have also compromised thousands of smaller employers, who have let people go, reluctantly and with great sadness, one at a time, victimized by languishing local markets for their goods and services. Some have survived, leaner and meaner against their will. Many, however, have not. Bankruptcies among small businesses in Canada did not decline after the recession ended, despite a public outcry against the banks for their stringent policies on small-business loans. Perhaps that outcry should also have taken aim at the corporations who are unconcerned when local economies "fail a bit."

The anger might also have been directed at governments who caught the downsizing fever spread by Canada's corporate global warriors. After years of great public enthusiasm for reducing the size of the public service, Canadians are noticing that drastic cuts have a negative impact on their local economies, and, therefore, on themselves.

When, for example, the Progressive Conservative government in Ontario announced in April 1996 that it would eliminate more than 10,500 positions in two years—in addition to 1,800 cuts announced previously—it was fulfilling a Common Sense Revolution promise that had swept the neoconservative government of Mike Harris into power a year earlier. However, after the details of the radical downsizing were announced—just days after the settlement of a lengthy and divisive civil-service strike undertaken by the Ontario Public Service Employees Union primarily to improve the severance entitlements and bumping rights of those whose jobs were about to disappear—the potential economic consequences of the cuts began to hit home.

Predictably, Opposition politicians warned that the massive cuts would drive the provincial economy—growing at a respectable annual rate of 2.7 per cent at the time—back into recession. But opposition to the cuts from Ontarians—including many who had voted for the government—was more widespread than Harris and Management Board chairman David Johnson might have expected. Within days of the announcement, the Tories began to lose support in opinion polls, and both the liberal *Toronto Star* and the conservative *Globe and Mail* ran lengthy series on the growing miseries of the middle classes.

The corporate community had its say too. Shortly after the extent of the cuts was made public, Aron Gampel, a senior economist at the Bank of Nova Scotia, told the *Star* that there was no question that such massive job losses would "take a toll on confidence, on spending and on the over-all performance" of the economy. "We are taking potential consumers out of the economic stream," Gampel conceded; but, he added, the economy "will suffer [in the] near term" to "secure gains in the long term." This is the corporate mantra of the nineties, most often articulated by spokesmen like the well-meaning Mr. Gampel, whose businesses are doing just fine.

Federal Finance minister Paul Martin often repeats another job-killing corporate mantra: "If a government doesn't need to run something, it shouldn't"—a dangerous imperative for institutions charged with safeguarding the interests of the citizenry. In corporate terms, "need" is invariably defined in terms of profit: Organizations should concentrate on what they do or make, the argument goes, and get out of costly auxiliary functions that have accrued over time, by "outsourcing" jobs. You have cleaners on the payroll? Fire them and hire a cleaning company. You have people offering training courses on the payroll? Fire them and hire consultants to train new employees and help existing employees retool, or do without. You have retirement-planning advisers on your payroll? Fire them and direct your employees to private firms.

In the public sector, however, outsourcing can reduce governments' ability to moderate the excesses and inequities of the marketplace by turning the hen house over to the fox, and those who advocate doing so usually have another, more ominous, message as well: that every potentially profitable government-run service—from health care to correctional facilities, to universities, to environmental agencies—should be given to the private sector.

Moreover, although outsourcing can make good sense, both for employers, who may not be capable of providing some services efficiently and cost-effectively, and for employees, who may get better advice from an outside adviser, better training from an external course, better food from an external caterer than from the company-run cafeteria, it can have adverse effects as well. Those whose jobs disappear in outsourcing exercises usually find themselves worse off. If they find jobs with the company contracted to do their jobs, they will, in most cases, earn less and have fewer benefits. If they enjoyed the protection of a union, they will, in most cases, lose it and/or seniority.

In corporate terms, this diminution in the quality of jobs is, of course, one point of the exercise. Former employers save money because they no longer have to provide pension plans and benefits packages. New employers make money because they don't provide them either. Thus, incomes fall, jobs deteriorate, expectations decline, and personal safety nets fray, even though the work remains, and, in some cases, so do the workers.

Moreover, taxpayers pay for such corporate efficiencies. It is not uncommon for employers to shift workers from employment status to contract positions in order to reduce costs. As the Canadian Payroll Association, which represents professional organizations that provide payroll services to employers, has pointed out, employers are not required to pay Canada Pension Plan or unemployment insurance premiums—or other benefits, such as disability and life insurance, to which they traditionally contributed—for employees classified as contract workers. This shedding of responsibility, in turn, can put workers and their families at risk, making them more likely to require assistance from the state at some time in their lives. In addition, contract workers, because they are classified for tax purposes as self-employed, and are therefore entitled to claim more deductions, will pay less tax than an employee earning the same wage. Thus do the heavy burdens of the corporations migrate to workers'—and to taxpayers'—shoulders.

Just as there are alternatives to the "global" model that are appropriate for large multinational corporations—and measures other than corporate profits by which to judge the performance of our economy—so too are there alternatives to outsourcing everything from photocopying to financial planning. The most obvious is to teach those about to be fired to do jobs remaining to be done. It won't work in every case, because some jobs will always be done better by those with specific and particular talents, or equipment, or training. But in most cases, the rush to outsource assumes that those about to lose their jobs are incapable of doing new work; it also fails to consider the possibility that their talents might have been misused or underused in the first place. From this point of view, outsourcing, like radical downsizing, is evidence that the employer, not the employee, has failed.

So, too, is the extreme rhetoric of corporate apologists' evidence of the dehumanized vision of the downsizing, contracting-out culture. In January 1996, for example, *Fortune*, one of the corporate bibles, ran a "Leading Edge" column entitled "Taking on the Last Bureaucracy" in which columnist Thomas A. Stewart offered this intemperate piece of advice about outsourcing: "Nestled warm and sleepy in your company, like the asp in Cleopatra's bosom, is a department whose employees spend 80% of their time on routine administrative tasks. Nearly every function of this department can be performed more expertly for less by others," Stewart wrote. "I am describing, of course, your human resources department, and have a modest proposal. Why not blow the sucker up. I don't mean improve HR. Improvement is for wimps. I mean abolish it. Deep six it. Rub it out; eliminate, toss, obliterate, nuke it; give it the old heave-ho, force it to walk the plank, turn it into road kill."

Perhaps Stewart's pseudo-Swiftian advice—seriously meant if hyperbolically offered—was useful to his readers; perhaps it wasn't. But that is hardly the point. The point is that the rhetorical excesses—as well as the realities—of workplace change have gotten down and dirty in the nineties. The good news is that there are signs that corporate leaders seem finally to be getting the message that their insensitive words, like their insensitive acts, not only are offensive, but may also be counter-productive. The savviest of them are making deliberate decisions to soften their language, to tone down the global-speak, to rein in the techno-determinist imagery that has caused pain to so many people. Some are even repudiating their leaner, meaner strategies as discredited approaches to workplace renewal that do not work, and never did.

This, however, does not mean that all of them will change their ways. Their leaders may be uncomfortable with the criticisms directed their way, but their personal discomfort will not change the fact that corporations were put on this earth for one reason: to make money, first for their executives, then for their shareholders. Nor will it relieve corporate pressure on government to eliminate civil-service jobs in order to make Canada competitive with low-wage third-world countries. The days when corporate leaders acted in ways that benefited society out of nothing more than a general sense of social responsibility unrelated to the bottom line are long gone, if they ever existed.

But one message does capture their attention: They may be shooting themselves in that bottom line when they drastically deplete their human capital, ignoring the consequences of their actions for the communities in which they operate. Compassion, social responsibility, and concern for local economies may be irrelevant to many who make corporate policy in the nineties, but corporate self-interest most decidedly is not.

One piece of advice that recently caught their attention is an observation that appears on the cover of the best-selling management book *Grow to Be Great: Breaking the Downsizing Cycle*, by U.S. management consultants Dwight Gertz and Joao Baptista. "You can't shrink to greatness," Gertz and Baptista warn in a tagline memorable precisely because it so neatly captures the aggressive, global-warrior mind-set of the nineties, in which bigger is better when it comes to new technologies and new territories to conquer, but not when it comes to people.

Our very own global warrior, the miller, has had a very effective audience with the King and his courtiers in the nineties. Clearly, those who have framed Canada's economic policies in the last decade have found his words persuasive. But it is by no means obvious to everyone in the kingdom that the miller can deliver on his promises. On the contrary, there are many who see no reason to believe that his daughter, although beautiful, truly does know how to spin straw into gold.

Chapter 3
Techno-Determinism and a Lost Generation

The little man ... sat down in front of the wheel. Turn, turn, turn, three times, and the bobbin was full.... And so it went—turn, turn, turn, all night long, until all the straw was spun and all the bobbins were full of gold.

Let us, for a moment, consider the spinning-wheel. Perhaps the King's spinning-wheel was a magical machine, capable of spinning straw into gold. Perhaps the miller's daughter, had she but known it, could have spun the King's straw into gold. Perhaps because she had never been asked to spin straw into gold, it did not occur to her that no matter who sat in front of the magic wheel, the straw would be spun into gold.

Or perhaps the bobbins were magical, transforming rough straw into supple, shining golden threads. Or perhaps it was just an ordinary spinning-wheel, such as her mother, and her mother's mother, had used to spin raw wool into yarn. What if there was nothing magical about the wheel, or the bobbins, at all?

Let us say that this spinning-wheel was not a magic wheel, or

the same wheel that her mother, and her mother's mother before
her, had used to spin wool into yarn. Let us say that the bobbins
were not magical either. How, then, was the straw changed into
gold?

Perhaps the straw was not changed into gold at all, but only
seemed to be so?

Imagine that!

The Freudian philosopher Herbert Marcuse suggested more
than thirty years ago that capitalism is not only an economic system but also a philosophy of life—a way of looking at the world based on a rigidly determinist approach to
nature and humanity that takes for granted that all human
problems are open to technological solutions. Marcuse
called this philosophy "technological rationality" and
observed that what little debate exists within its framework
inevitably focuses not on the ends of human society but on
the expansion of capitalism itself.

When technological rationality drives society, Marcuse
said, thought becomes one-dimensional and non-critical,
and it is taken for granted that social institutions, such as
work, *must* be organized in ways that exploit—rather than
nurture—human beings and natural resources. Modern
capitalism, he observed, "swamps all potential criticism in a
sea of commodities," and measures the good life in the
ownership of an ever-increasing supply of material goods. It
also, he noted, measures the worth of people in terms of
their immediate usefulness to the capitalist enterprise, not
in terms of human self-actualization and democracy.

We are living in techno-rationalist times. After more
than a decade of radical, market-driven reform, however,
we might wish to ponder Marcuse's words, in the hope that
they may lead us to new ways of understanding the
changes that are taking place in the ways we work and in
the work we do. We might also wish to ponder the human
consequences of these reforms. As voters, we have placed
the future of Canada in the hands of politicians whose eco-

nomic policies are driven by the overriding goal of reducing public indebtedness as rapidly as possible. In pursuing the laudable aim of fiscal responsibility, however, these politicians, with little debate and less consultation, have accepted on our behalf the fundamental premise of technical rationality: that an unfettered market is the *only* solution to Canada's economic and social problems, now and in the future.

Dalton Camp is the always-thoughtful Progressive Conservative insider who advised Brian Mulroney in the 1984 "Jobs, Jobs, Jobs" campaign. Now deeply disenchanted with the Reaganite policies of the government he helped elect, Camp has provided us with a fine description of the ideological fervour gripping Canadian politicians. "When governments become prisoners of their own lack of vision," Camp wrote in his *Toronto Star* column in April 1996, "they ascribe to themselves heroic attributes. They advertise themselves as 'toughing it out,' resolve to 'stay the course' and preen themselves on 'being on the right track.' The people are overwhelmed by official unanimity and are given no alternatives or contradictory opinion. The sterile, fixated war on the deficit is trench warfare fought by today's generals in suits, firing statistics. No matter the cost or the casualties, they know they're right."

A philosophical commitment to diminishing the role of government, in the belief that the freer the marketplace, the more prosperous the society, has always been one magnetic pole of the political dynamic that gives democratic, industrialized nations balance. Throughout our history, Canadians have debated the appropriate role of government in our mixed economy with great vigour, and this debate has more often than not stood us in very good stead. In the last decade, however, the dynamic has lost its equilibrium.

"We Have No Alternative" has echoed through the land, effectively silencing debate on alternative courses of action. Those who have dissented from debt- and deficit-obsessed government policies are dismissed. They are ridiculed by neoconservative economists and gleeful right-wing columnists as fools, trapped in the miasma of the "lunatic left," whose views have been discredited not only by high levels of public indebtedness but also by the collapse of the Soviet Union, the rapid pace of technological change, and the rise of the global economy.

Consider, for example, the reception accorded Toronto writer Linda McQuaig's 1995 book, *Shooting the Hippo: Death by Deficit and Other Canadian Myths*, by the mainstream business press. In her carefully researched attack on the corporate orthodoxy of the nineties, McQuaig posited the deliberate repression by corporate interests of dialogue on alternative economic strategies. She explored in careful detail the ways in which corporate interests had circumscribed and influenced policy decisions out of sight of Canadian voters. Her arguments, persuasive and well documented, were, of course, open to debate and criticism, as every argument is and should be. By and large, however, the book was, instead, dismissed out of hand by reviewers inside the corporate loop. "McQuaig appears either to ignore the increasingly integrated nature of the global economy or to feel that Canada can function as an economic outlaw," sniffed Anthony Wilson-Smith in a *Maclean's* review typical of the genre.

As subsequent events would show, McQuaig was more right than wrong. The pace of technological, economic, and geopolitical change, together with widespread public confusion about these changes, would continue to provide corporate interests with the perfect cover for engineering massive shifts in Canada's traditional political dynamic. Almost without our noticing it, the corporate imperative—to scale back government ruthlessly, to reduce its regulative authority, to devolve its powers—became our imperative too.

Civil servants? Why do we need them? Don't they just push paper and get in the way? Stricter, and better enforcement of, environmental standards? Why do we need controls at all? Haven't we solved the worst of the problems? More effective regulation of financial institutions? Aren't our banks among the best and most stable in the world? And so on. On the one hand, we had become a society increasingly unhappy with the our governments' lack of progress in creating jobs and in helping us cope in a fast-changing and rapidly shrinking workplace. On the other, many of us had become perversely enthusiastic supporters of policies that by their very nature trivialized and dismissed these very concerns.

Why did so many of us buy into the deficit-busting, profit-driven corporate imperative? Why did so many of us simply agree with the proposition that the best government is no government, even when to do so was also to accept its corollary: that market forces alone are sufficient to govern our lives? Why has the debate in the nineties been conducted almost exclusively within the iron grip of Marcuse's technological rationality?

One reason is that many of us are deeply frightened by the rapid and fundamental changes transforming our workplaces. We know that the technology now exists to create a "global" economy—already more than half of the largest economies in the world are corporations—and we are scared out of our wits that we will miss the global economic boat if we defy those who hold our tickets. At the same time we are terrified that the very technology that drives the new economy will determine—and change forever—how we think, how we work, and how we live our lives.

When pollster Allan Gregg looked at the results of *Maclean's* annual year-end poll in January 1996, he reported that they were "the blackest" he had ever seen. In his overview of the poll, Gregg wrote that at the end of 1995, Canadians believed overwhelmingly that "virtually everything about Canada not only has got worse than it was in times past, a condition we have witnessed in other research findings, but that we can expect continued deterioration as we move into the future." That tendency, Gregg observed, "is foreign not only to past research findings, but to the very underpinnings of our popular culture." He added, with obvious regret, that the "areas where this deterioration is anticipated most are the same ones that best define Canadians' unique sense of national identity and self: our social programs and social fabric, the opportunities for advancement afforded to our young people, and our economic prosperity."

Although the poll was designed to focus primarily on Canadians' attitudes towards the Quebec government's wish to separate from Canada, it nevertheless found that "an outright majority—56 per cent" of those polled said that economic concerns, not Quebec's separatist ambitions and Canada's future as a nation, were of "paramount" concern to them. "Canadians report that not only is their outlook for the future negative," Gregg observed, but that they believe the "aspects of Canadian life that have given us a common sense of purpose and character will exist—if at all—only as pale imitations of what they were."

It is perhaps ironic that Allan Gregg was also the official pollster for the Mulroney government, which first inflicted on us a rigid, neoconservative mind-set, because it seems clear from his essay that he would now agree that the techno-determinism of the corporate global vision has not been entirely good for our economic—or our psychological—well-being. As the *Maclean's* poll confirmed, that agenda has caused us to believe that we are losing all control over the forces that govern our lives. It has also caused us to believe that our politicians are paralysed by circumstances, and have no real choices on economic policy. It has caused us to believe that our *society* has no real choices, that we are in the midst of an economic cataclysm that we have no hope of mitigating.

Corporate techno-determinism has also convinced many of us that the societal goals we held in common only a decade or so ago are no longer achievable because the scale of the global economy is sweeping us into oblivion. More damaging, it has caused us to accept without question the corporate argument that the only way we can hope to thrive in the future is to make our governments, especially our federal government, much smaller and radically reduced in power, thereby allowing corporations to become much larger, freer, and more profitable, no matter the cost to society.

Contrast this agenda with a gentler view of technological and workplace change, once commonly held but now effectively swamped by deficit obsession. Sooner or later, the scenario goes, technology will reverse the ratio of work and leisure: We will spend less time working because there will be less work to be done. This reversal will not only change the way we live our daily lives, but also allow us to focus our attention on other, non-work aspects of our lives. Freed from the daily tyranny of the workplace, we will have more time and energy for families and friends, more time to reflect, more time to be responsible citizens, more time to do whatever we wish to do. We will, in Marcuse's terms, cease to measure our accomplishments by our jobs, and cease to define the good life in terms of an ever-increasing supply of material goods.

In the nineties, this scenario seems more Utopian and less possible than at any time in the last fifty years. Whereas earlier technological advances reduced the average number of hours most people worked, the computer and computer-related technology have had little impact on the length of a standard work week. In the United States, for example, productivity has more than doubled since 1948 and, as Jeremy Rifkin has pointed out, Americans can produce their 1948 standard of living in less than half the time it took them in that year. Yet today the work week in the United States is roughly the same length it was in 1960: More than 25 per cent of all full-time workers log forty-nine or more hours on the job each week, and the average American receives fewer paid vacation days than in the early seventies. In Canada, in the last four decades, the typical workload has increased 40 per cent, effectively reducing leisure time and steadily adding one additional day of work each year.

These statistics, of course, do not mean that new technologies *increase* the time it takes to do the work that needs to be done. On the contrary, Canadian futurist John Kettle estimated in his "Kettle's Future" column in the *Globe and Mail* on April 20, 1996, that if all the work to be done in Canada today were allocated evenly over the workforce among those currently working and those looking for employment, our work week would average barely thirty hours. How is it, then, that we confront an apparent paradox, in which more efficient means of production are translating into longer working hours?

The statistics are not really paradoxical at all, of course. They are, rather, indications of inequities in ways work is distributed. Many full-time workers are working longer and harder; many others, being unemployed, are not working at all. In between are legions of Canadians who are seriously, and possibly permanently, underemployed. These people, to be sure, have a surfeit of time on their hands, but it is not leisure time: For the unemployed and the underemployed, the equation that time equals leisure is meaningless. Lacking adequate income to provide a satisfactory quality of life, they are trapped by the ways technology is being put to use, without regard for its human consequences, and without regard for the well-being of society.

In short, what has changed in postmodern industrial societies, including Canada, is that traditional understandings between employees and employers, and between governments and their citizens, have been abandoned for the demands, real or imagined, of the global marketplace. Until recently, high unemployment in Western countries was considered to be a *shared* problem—a failure of government, and of society in general, to address economic problems that undermine the quality of life for everyone. In the nineties, many of us have come to see government as the cause of, not the solution to, these problems, just as many of us have come to see the poor as the self-selected authors of their own misfortunes.

John Kenneth Galbraith has described this change in perception in terms of the widening income gap between the financially comfortable and the poor in most Western societies. "The great dialectic used to be between capital and labor," Galbraith noted in a 1993 round-table discussion organized by *Mother Jones* magazine. "Today, the conflict is between the comfortable and the deprived. The comfortable have come to see government as the threat because it is the only hope for the deprived." In the three years since Galbraith made that observation, unemployment has transformed more of the "comfortable" into the "deprived," further fuelling the inclination of the comfortable who remain to see governments, and the social programs they administer, as a threat to their own well-being.

How else to explain, to take just one example, most Ontarians' docile acceptance of their Conservative government's decision to cut welfare rates by 21.6 per cent at a time when jobs were disappearing, as though the recession had never ended. As the Toronto writer Heather Robertson put it succinctly in her 1995 *Globe and Mail* review of *Straight Through the Heart*, Maude Barlow and Bruce Campbell's examination of the "slash-and burn" corporate ideology: "[The book] ignores the most curious phenomenon arising from deficit-slashing; people love it, even those being 'downsized.'"

Ralph Klein "has become a folk hero, Chrétien's popularity is undiminished, and support for Ontario's Common Sense Revolution rose to 50 per cent after Premier Mike Harris promised to cut welfare," Robertson noted, asking, "Are we dupes? Masochists? Puritans?" There is "a certain satisfaction to be found in making do with less," she added. "Environmentalism poses a more powerful threat to consumerism than socialism—and people may hate their jobs so much they prefer to work part-time or not at all. Perhaps we are all so fed up with government we'd just as soon go it alone."

Robertson's comments were bang on. But that was then and this is now, and perceptions are changing. As the effects of "slash and burn" have drifted from economic theory into the reality of our daily lives, Canadians are becoming increasingly sceptical about the wisdom of the pace of change demanded by the radical debt- and deficit-slashing corporate imperative. They are also becoming increasingly angered by the refusal of federal and provincial governments to keep their promises to seriously pursue more creative and humane solutions to the growing inequities in the job market, especially in the job market for younger Canadians.

Before we examine the human consequences of this failure in more detail, we must take a brief look at a few statistics, just to put things in perspective. Please don't glaze over; it's important to get a general picture of the jobs situation in Canada today—it may not be quite what you think it is—to understand how the workplace is changing, and to enable us to think about one of the themes of this book: that new policies that balance debt and deficit reduction with job creation could make a real difference to our lives. We will revisit all these figures later in the book in a fuller context, but, for now, let's glance at some of the most telling workplace statistics of the mid-nineties.

- In mid-1996, according to the official numbers issued by Statistics Canada (the source for all these figures, unless otherwise indicated), more than 1.5 million Canadians were out of work, an unemployment rate of 10 per cent. Because so many people have given up looking for work, however, this "official" count is at least half a million shy of the actual number unemployed. Canada's "unofficial unemployment rate"—measured by pre-recession workplace-participation standards—is 13 per cent, or even higher.

- In 1995, a third of all Canadian families reported at least one wage-earner out of work.
- Between 1982 and 1990, a time of high economic growth, three of every four new jobs in Canada were full-time. Since 1990, just one in four has been full-time.
- Nearly 20 per cent of all jobs in Canada today are part-time, up from 12.5 per cent in 1976, and from 16.6 per cent in 1989. More than 2.5 million Canadians are now working part-time. Of these, 33 per cent—compared with 20 per cent in 1990, and 10 per cent in 1976—report that they have settled for part-time work solely because they cannot find full-time jobs.
- Overwhelmingly, part-time jobs are filled by women. Today, women make up 45 per cent of Canada's work-force, but they comprise 69 per cent of all part-time workers. About 28 per cent of working women hold part-time jobs, as do 11 per cent of working men.
- Almost half the jobs created in Canada in the last twenty years have been "non-standard" jobs—part-time, temporary, or contract positions—most without pensions, benefits, or job security. In the nineties, non-standard jobs account for about 30 per cent of all employment in Canada.
- The increase in part-time, non-standard work has impacted most seriously on young Canadians. In 1995, 45 per cent of working Canadians between the ages of fifteen and twenty-four held part-time jobs, up from 21 per cent in 1976, and from 33 per cent in the late eighties.
- For those with high-school education or less, there were 997,000 *fewer* jobs in 1995 than in 1990, while for those with at least some postsecondary education, there were 1.2 million *more* jobs in 1995 than in 1990, still not enough to provide work for at least 7 per cent of educated young Canadians.
- The sector creating the most jobs in Canada today is what Statistics Canada calls the "community, business

and personal services" category. Usually called the "service sector," it accounts for about four in every ten jobs across the country and has supplied nearly 70 per cent of all new jobs since the recession ended officially in 1992.

Taken together, these trends raise serious concerns about Canada's changing workplace, in both the short and the long term, and we will address them all in due course. For now, let's consider the effect high unemployment—and the high underemployment reflected in the dramatic shift from full- to part-time, non-standard jobs—will have on young Canadians entering the workplace in the nineties and on the long-term durability of Canada's social fabric.

In advanced industrial societies such as ours, the work people do—their "occupations"—has traditionally been a fundamental link between individuals and the larger social structure. Occupations have determined, for better or for worse, the nature of many human social interactions with others occupying similar, subordinate, or superordinate roles, and with clients and customers. They have linked us with other people beyond our own private worlds, in a systematic and understandable way. Occupations, for better or for worse, have also been a major source of personal identity. This has been particularly true in advanced industrial societies such as Canada that are characterized by geographical mobility and in which the nuclear family, however defined, has largely supplanted the extended family. In short, our "occupations" have always had a profound and direct effect on our lives.

Now, we are told, the "occupation," like the "career," is disappearing forever. Not only is technology making many low-skill occupations redundant, it is also changing the nature of skilled work: New tasks, requiring split-second deployment of human resources, emerge overnight. In *The End of Work*, Jeremy Rifkin describes what is happening to unskilled workers: "The high-tech global economy is moving beyond the mass worker. While entrepreneurial, managerial, professional, and technical elites will be necessary to run the formal economy of the future, fewer and fewer workers will be required to assist in the production of goods and services." The market value of labour is diminishing, Rifkin says, and will continue to do so. "After centuries of defining human worth in strictly 'productive' terms, the wholesale replacement of human labor with machine labor leaves the mass worker without self-definition or societal function."

U.S. management consultant William Bridges, whose clients include Intel, Bell, Apple, and Procter & Gamble, includes skilled workers in his analysis: The "job," he says, in his influential book *Job Shift: How to Prosper in a Workplace without Jobs*, is disappearing. "Today's transformation is so large that you have to go back almost two centuries to the coming of industrialism to find a comparable change." During that earlier period, Bridges observes, "work was packaged into 'jobs' to fit the demands of a new kind of workplace, and the numbers of those jobs grew along with the appearance of large factories and bureaucracies." In our own time, he points out, "those big workplaces are shrinking and being automated, and work is once again being repackaged to meet new economic realities." Not only are "careers" and "occupations" disappearing, Bridges says, but so are jobs, "this time for good."

Bridges notes that the private company that employed more Americans than any other in 1993, the year before *Job Shift* was published, was the temporary-employment agency Manpower. With 560,000 employees, it dwarfed such corporate giants as General Motors (365,000 employees) and IBM (330,000 employees). America, he says, is being "temped" with "contingent" or "just-in-time" workers doing everything from clerical work to benefits analysis to systems engineering. Some companies, he adds, have done away with permanent employees altogether; instead, they "lease" their workers from temp agencies.

But there is another reason "occupations" and "jobs" are

disappearing: People who want "careers" and "occupations" and "jobs" are detrimental to profits. After all, "career" and "occupation" are old-fashioned words that imply a two-way relationship of trust and responsibility between employers and employees; they also require a measure of security to flourish. Instead, employers in the nineties insist that the future of work will offer no security and no trust; virtually everyone will be self-employed, carrying their skills in a little kit-bag to be deployed when and if an employer has a "task" to be discharged, and packed up again when the assignment has been completed.

The world beyond jobs, Bridges observes, has both advantages and costs. "It offers more freedom, more control over one's time, more consistency with personal values, more self-expression, more flexibility, more chance to see the results of one's labors." But it also, he notes, "exposes people to non-stop change, has all the economic instability of self-employment, and can magnify self-doubt and disorganized habits." Moreover, "it destroys the sense of community that existed in many workplaces," Bridges notes wistfully, "and so it can be very lonely.... I worry that without the counterweight of a solid sense of self and a clear grasp of personal values, individuals will not be able to withstand the centrifugal forces of the market. People willing to become whatever market opportunities will pay them to be either get pulled apart or become centerless, lacking any overriding purpose."

This would seem to be an accurate description of what is happening to many Canadians, especially young Canadians. It is certainly true that many people enjoy self-employment enormously—I count myself among them—just as it is true that contract work has long been the norm in many professions. But young people today seem persuaded both that the old world has vanished and that the world replacing it holds no promise for them. They are told that there is no point in aiming for a "career," or in preparing themselves for an "occupation." They are told that it is

impossible to predict the "jobs" of the future and are therefore urged to prepare themselves to be all things to all
employers—primarily, it would seem, by honing their computer skills and remaining in school as long as possible.

And what are they offered in return? The prospect of a
significant decline in their standard of living, a lifetime of
toting their kit-bags of skills from employer to employer, a
shredded safety net too weak to break their fall in bad
times, and governments determined to scare them witless
with the monster of debts and deficits. Can it be any wonder that many of them see themselves as a "lost generation," abandoned by the global warriors marching off to
make fortunes in the wider world.

William Bridges is in the business of advising corporations how to restructure their operations, so it is interesting
that he chooses not to dwell on the possibility that this
brave new world is emerging primarily because employers
have made deliberate decisions that it should. By and large,
corporations in the nineties have decided to "contract out"
to save money, and thereby generate profit. They may boast
that the new workplace improves the prospects for "con-
sistent self-expression" and "flexibility" of the employees
they have let go or don't intend to hire, but they don't seem
too concerned about "destroyed senses of community" or
"concerted assaults on personal identity." These consequences are apparently an insignificant price to pay for
cost-efficiencies.

But are they? What of the young people who are told
that they should expect to "temp" in the new economy? If
they are highly skilled, and their skills are in demand, they
will likely earn enough from their contracts to compensate
for what they have lost: pension plans, benefits packages, a
chance for advancement in the workplace, and a measure
of job security. Indeed, those with highly marketable
skills—and temperaments that can withstand "a little lone-
liness"—will probably do just fine in the global economy.
We would be wise to encourage them to acquire such skills

so that their bulging kit-bags will enable them to thrive and prosper.

But what about the majority of "temporary workers," young people who are ambitious, competent, and skilled, but whose skills are not extraordinary? For them, the situation looks different. I recently observed the world of the "temporary" worker as my twenty-three-year-old Australian nephew, armed with a commerce degree, experience in hotel catering, a one-year work permit, and indefatigable job-hunting skills, worked as long as he was needed with one Canadian employer before moving on to the next. Because he is an uncommonly gregarious and charming person, and because he had no possibility of working for more than a year in Canada, this routine suited him well, although he would have preferred a "regular" job related to what he would like to do in life, and a little more in wages.

First he worked as a telemarketer, selling accident- and life-insurance policies across Canada, in places he had never heard of but was pleased to discover, for $8 an hour, plus the occasional bonus. Next, he toiled at Citibank, verifying preapproved Citibank Visa-card applications from across the country, for $8.50 an hour, plus the occasional bonus. Then, he moved to the Immigration and Refugee Board, photocopying, filing, typing, word processing, and shifting boxes of records, for $8 an hour. From there, he moved to Bell Canada's Competitive Business Practices Team, where things looked up. Not only did the job pay $10 an hour (but no bonuses), it also lasted longer than the others, largely by virtue of his own self-promotion. It was even vaguely related to his academic training and career aspirations.

Two things intrigued me about Matthew's sojourn in the world of temporary work. The first was that there is no shortage of this kind of work, in Toronto at least. The second was trying to imagine how anyone could survive it for long. Not only was the pay very low, but employment was spotty at best. Jobs disappear literally overnight, and people are told to leave early, without pay, when there is no work to be done. Some of the telemarketing jobs had particularly Draconian bonus and demerit systems, the rules of which changed daily, as fresh geographical areas to prospect opened up and exhausted ones closed down. There must have been some logic to these bonus systems, but their inscrutability meant that not only was there no job security, there was also no wage security *within* the job. Indeed, sometimes it was impossible to know how much one was earning until the paycheque arrived, reflecting mysteriously calculated bonuses awarded and demerits imposed.

It is instructive to contrast the realities of part-time, temporary work with the reassuring rhetoric of the apologists for the downsizing, outsourcing tactics of corporations and the deficit-cutting economic policies of governments. John Geddes, who writes the "Inside Ottawa" column in *The Financial Post*, for example, declared in May 1996 that the federal Liberals were "musing privately about possible tax cuts or new programs becoming affordable" before the next election. "This new flexibility," Geddes declared, "comes without anything like the upheaval and privation predicted by those who opposed deficit reduction." No upheaval? No privation? What planet, pray tell, is Mr. Geddes living on?

Such disinformation, dispensed as gospel truth, is symptomatic of what may be the biggest single problem with workplace change. The economic indicators can be stellar for many of us and dismal for many others. We are still extremely confused: Are we simply trying to put our economic house in order by driving debt down, or are we trying to cope with catastrophic workplace change that will not go away no matter how many government balance sheets tip over into the black? This confusion—between deep structural change and cyclical economic change—has blinded us to how thoroughly employers have seized the opportunity provided by government deficits to offload their traditional responsibilities.

When the boosters of corporate Canada look at the world they have created and declare confidently that it is good, they deeply offend all those Canadians who are struggling to keep their lives on track. They also deeply offend all of us who believe that governments have an obligation to use our taxes to buffer those who lose their livelihoods in times of economic upheaval, not to reduce support to them while suggesting that it is their own fault that they are in need. Similarly, they deeply damage all the young Canadians who have lost hope of ever finding a decent job, of ever experiencing a time when some things, if not all things, are fine.

Despite what they are told by corporate apologists and global warriors, many older Canadians know that things are not fine—that as government cut-backs trickle down to local municipalities, the upheavals in our society are just beginning. When governments abandon education, gut community services, turn their backs on the arts, denature environmental protections, and weaken the laws that protect us in the workplace, we can take little solace in the economic good news that so cheers John Geddes. Yet we want desperately to believe that we are through the worst of it. We want to hear that corporations are hiring, that the economy is on the upswing, and that deficits are sufficiently under control that Canada is no longer at the mercy of international money markets and U.S. inflation rates.

Many of us, however, remain deeply sceptical about the trustworthiness of corporations who are remaking our lives and staying the moderating hand of government. We are concerned that their spinning-wheel is not magical at all, just a costly, well-marketed device that spins ordinary fleece into ordinary wool. We are concerned that the bobbins are not magical either, though they may have seemed so to the miller's daughter. We are concerned that there are those who wish to spin straw into gold, not for all the people of the kingdom, but for only a few.

Part 2

Chapter 4
Global Visions, Local Miseries

*"Tonight, you must spin this straw into gold,"
the King said. "But when you have completed
your task, your labours will be over and you
shall be my wife...."*

*In her difficulty, the miller's daughter said
to herself, How can I know that the King speaks
the truth? How can I know that I shall be his
wife?*

Let us, for a moment, consider the miller's daughter. Was she persuaded to take part in her father's ruse because she believed he
meant no harm, that he meant only to gain the King's ear? Or did
she not know her father intended to tell the King his daughter
could spin his straw into gold?

Perhaps she went with him to the palace simply to pass the time
of day, or to glimpse the many splendours of the court.

What, then, did she feel when she was locked in the King's
room and ordered to spin the straw into gold before morning?
What, then, did she feel when the little man appeared before her?

Terror? Relief? Gratitude?

Let us say that the miller's daughter had no idea her father would tell the King she had magical powers. Let us say also that she despaired in the locked room, and was both relieved and grateful when the little man appeared, offering to spin the straw into gold.

Little did she know, however, that although the King may have been an honourable man, Rumpelstiltskin intended to demand a high price for his labours, for he knew she would become Queen.

Imagine that!

"One of the most significant human commitments of the last half of this century has been to economic growth and trade expansion, and we have been spectacularly successful in accomplishing both," wrote the international-development expert David Korten in his 1995 book, *When Corporations Rule the World*. Global economic output, Korten notes, "expanded from $3.8 trillion in 1950 to $18.9 trillion in 1992—a nearly fivefold increase; world trade soared from total exports of $308 billion to $3,554 billion—an 11.5-fold increase, or more than twice the rate of increase of total economic output." This means "that, on average, we have added more to total global output *in each of the past four decades* than was added from the moment the first cave dweller carved out a stone axe up to the middle of the present century."

We have reached a point in human history, Korten says, when it seems that we truly have the knowledge, technology, and organizational capacity to accomplish bold goals, including the elimination of poverty, war, and disease. The nineties, he observes, should be a time filled with hope for "a new millennium in which societies will be freed forever from concerns of basic survival and security to pursue new frontiers of social, intellectual, and spiritual advancement." Yet fewer and fewer people believe that their economic futures are secure. "Family and community units and the security they once provided are disintegrating," Korten says. "The natural environment on which we depend for our material needs is evaporating, and we find a profound and growing suspicion among thoughtful people the world over that something has gone very wrong."

Many other observers of the global marketplace are echoing Korten's concerns. They are deeply worried about the human consequences of globalization, and about the apparent inability of existing institutions to cope with such rapid and fundamental economic change. Growing numbers of environmentalists, philosophers, sociologists, economists, and disenchanted development experts, like Korten, are raising disturbing questions about such trends as the growing income gap between rich and poor; the threats growing concentration of corporate power poses to democratic institutions and national autonomy; and, perhaps most urgently, the havoc wreaked by global money markets on many national economies.

"Global corporations are the first secular institutions run by men (and a handful of women) who think and plan on a global scale," wrote Richard Barnet and John Cavanagh, in *Global Dreams: Imperial Corporations and the New World Order*, one of the many recent books that challenge corporate assurances that the new economy will inevitably lead to greater prosperity for all. They point out that the combined assets of the top three hundred multinational firms now make up roughly a quarter of the productive assets of the entire world. These giant companies with worldwide connections are effectively dominating the four intersecting webs of global commercial activity on which the new world economy largely rests: culture, goods, the workplace, and the global financial network. "These worldwide webs of economic activity have already achieved a degree of global integration never before achieved by any world empire or nation state," Barnet and Cavanagh warn, "and the driving force behind each of them can be traced in large measure to the same few hundred corporate giants."

The sheer scope of these criticisms, welcome as they are,

inevitably contributes to our collective feelings of power-lessness in the face of change. If the primary cause of Canada's current economic difficulties is the emergent global economy, how, we wonder, can we ever, as individuals, or even as a society, hope to exercise any control whatsoever over the events and forces that will determine our lives in the twenty-first century? To be sure, these books help us make sense of such macro-economic trends as global unemployment and free trade, and the concomitant resurgence of nationalism around the world; but, until recently, most of them have provided scant guidance on what we can do to mitigate the micro-economic dislocations that threaten us as individuals.

Nowhere is this truer than in analyses of the rise of integrated global financial systems. No single aspect of our ongoing economic difficulties has been more frustrating to Canadians than the dominating role international money markets are playing in our economy. The emergence of the electronic global financial market has made it increasingly difficult for most national governments, including our own, to formulate and carry out economic policy. More than $2 trillion a day travels electronically from one place to another virtually instantaneously, and the daily exchange of one currency for another can amount to hundreds of billions of dollars. Only about 10 per cent of such currency exchange, Barnet and Cavanagh point out, has anything at all to do with "normal commercial transactions." It is, rather, money on which someone, somewhere, is trying to make more, simply by moving it around.

John Maynard Keynes, an economist much out of favour with global warriors, foresaw what he called the "casino" economy more than half a century ago; but even he could not have predicted how technologically sophisticated the casino would become. Today, speculative financial transactions—which are nothing more than computerized gambling—are causing national governments to lose control of their economies. Because Canada, like many other countries, has had to borrow heavily on international markets to finance our debts, we are at the mercy of the global gamblers, whose objectives have nothing at all to do with the best interests of Canadians. This vulnerability to foreign borrowers has forced our central bank to pay high interest-rate premiums to attract their capital, just as it has forced our governments to make deficit reduction and inflation containment priorities.

In meeting those requirements, our governments have also served the interests of large multinational corporations at the expense of the millions of Canadians who are out of work. The corporate goading of government to reduce the deficit, even at the cost of so many jobs, has been supported by warnings from bank presidents and other corporate spokesmen about the evils of inflation. Although passionately delivered and eagerly received by many of us, however, much of their rhetoric was hypocritical bunk. The private sector in Canada lived quite happily with the moderately high inflation rates of the mid- and late eighties, in part because so many large employers were benefiting hugely from the economic climate of the day. It was during the eighties, after all, that many of them could thank a combination of high inflation and high interest rates for the millions of dollars they were making on company pension plans on the backs of their retired employees, whose real incomes were severely eroded by the very high inflation that created windfall profits for large corporate employers.

Similarly, although Canadian bankers have been urging Ottawa to attack inflation since the early seventies, for years we heard few corporate complaints about deficit financing. In part this was because governments were borrowing primarily from Canadian institutions and Canadian investors; but corporate leaders also knew full well that deficit spending is a standard way for governments to finance such investments in the future as infrastructure, research and development, and education. When inflation pushed the deficits to levels that forced many governments to borrow offshore, however, corporate attitudes suddenly changed. Now it was foreign lenders, not just Canadian creditors, who were profiting from government indebtedness, and foreign lenders who were dictating the terms of the loans by threatening to shift their business elsewhere.

As the country became more and more exposed to foreign markets (which, coincidentally, were being transformed by sophisticated new technologies that linked markets and investors in a vast global web), it became clear that Canadian capital markets were exceptionally vulnerable to the vagaries of global investors. Not only did the new technologies encourage the development of a range of highly speculative financial instruments, they also enabled financial transactions to be made in a split second, encouraging large institutional investors to shift their money in and out of national markets in search of short-term profit, and enabling speculators to develop ever-more-intricate strategies to profit from split-second shifts of billions of electronic dollars from one currency to another. All these factors were destabilizing the Canadian dollar.

As the deficits grew, it also became clear that it would be necessary for governments to work towards reducing them. This goal was not the issue, although many governments, including the Mulroney Tories, paid noisy lip-service to deficit reduction while piling up debt. The issue was the speed at which deficits should be reduced, and how governments should go about it. Early in this decade, with the country in a devastating recession, many governments saw that if the deficits continued to grow at their current rate—or even escalated as tax revenues declined and demands on social programs increased because of the recession—they would soon be bankrupt. They reacted ruthlessly, quickly, and thoroughly. But why so ruthlessly? And why so quickly? And why with so little attention to the causes of the mushrooming deficits and the consequences of policies that marginalized job creation?

Although these are large questions, the basic answer is

actually simple: Monetary instability is far more trouble-some to large corporations than are societal instability and human disruption. As David Korten puts it succinctly, "Corporations engaged in producing real goods and services prefer a stable and predictable financial system that pro-vides reliable sources of investment funds at stable exchange and interest rates. For them, fluctuations in the financial markets are sources of risk that may disrupt their operations and balance sheets with little warning."

Corporate leaders had another reason for targeting the deficits. They recognized that rising debt levels, combined with the ongoing campaign to wrestle inflation to the ground, presented them with an unprecedented opportu-nity to remake Canadian society in ways more to their lik-ing, and were quick to seize the advantage. Deficits per-ceived by most Canadians to be unacceptably high, and a debilitating recession, emboldened corporate leaders to launch a concerted and well-organized campaign—through such organizations as the Fraser Institute, the C.D. Howe Institute, the Business Council on National Issues, and the Canadian Bankers Association—to shift the centre point of Canada's traditional political dynamic several notches to the right.

Their goals, as always, were to make governments smaller and to reduce their regulative powers; to lower their own costs of doing business by attacking social pro-grams that cost them money, such as unemployment insur-ance and the Canada Pension Plan; and to remake their workplaces in ways that would reduce their payrolls and fatten their bottom lines. Simultaneously, they undertook a well-funded, and largely successful, public disinformation effort to persuade Canadians that "There Is No Alternative" to such measures, that we have no choice but to endure severe short-term pain for long-term gain.

But why, you might well ask, did our politicians, most of whom won election by promising Canadians "jobs, jobs, jobs," go along with an agenda clearly so destructive to jobs and social equity? The answer to that question is simple too. Both the Progressive Conservative government of Brian Mulroney, despite its election promises to create jobs and to protect the country's social programs, and the Liberal government of Jean Chrétien, despite its election promises to concentrate its energies on job creation—by rewriting the free-trade deal with the United States, for example—had swallowed the corporate arguments whole. Knowing, however, that Canadians would find them unacceptable, they kept their views to themselves until they had been elected. Once in power, they endorsed harsh corporate prescriptions for economic growth, fully aware that these measures would change the nature of Canadian society forever.

So effective were the doomsday scenarios of the deficit-busters that both debate on the pace of deficit reduction and organized political resistance to corporate pressure have been effectively stifled. At the federal level, the Bloc Québécois has another agenda; the Reform Party is in sympathy with many corporate goals, albeit often for socially regressive reasons; and the NDP, which could have forced debate on these critical questions, lost its credibility when Bob Rae and his NDP government in Ontario gambled with corporate appeasement and lost. Other provincial politicians—Liberal premier Frank McKenna in New Brunswick, and NDP premier Roy Romanow in Saskatchewan, among them—climbed aboard, although they too had campaigned on promises of job creation.

This political vacuum, which we created with our votes, has cost us dearly. The social programs that have disappeared, scapegoated to rapid deficit reduction, will never be back, nor will any pretence of maintaining the universality—and equity—of everything from health care to job training to unemployment benefits. Indeed, many Canadians have forgotten why universality "mattered." (It mattered because it was a safeguard: The financially comfortable tend to be more willing to contribute tax dollars to health care and social programs for those less fortunate

ple, too. They would do so because they are committed to redirecting all the money that currently flows into the plan into capital markets, safely out of the control of the federal government. Although they don't dwell on it, they would also like to relieve themselves, as employers, of the "burden" of having to contribute to the plan on behalf of their employees.

The baldest suggestion for reforming the CPP was delivered by *The Globe and Mail*'s front-line global warrior, Andrew Coyne, who took a shine to the government of Chile's decision to boost its economy a decade and a half ago by forcing its citizens to invest their retirement savings in the stock market. "In 1982," Coyne wrote in August 1994, "the government of Chile privatized the country's pension plan. Every individual is now required to put at least 10 per cent of his or her salary into a tax-sheltered, individual retirement account, from which a pension will eventually be paid." Rather than "being dumped into a centrally administered fund," Coyne explained enthusiastically, "the money remains in separate accounts, which a number of private investment funds compete to manage." Canada should consider doing the same, he urged, because simply reforming the Canada Pension Plan would force employers to continue to finance it through "a job-killing payroll tax." Wouldn't it be better if "each and every citizen" were assigned the "personal responsibility to save for his or her own retirement."

The Chrétien government stopped short of endorsing the Chilean model, but in February 1995, Finance minister Paul Martin announced that the CPP was in serious difficulties and required immediate attention. The plan was in trouble, he said, because "disability benefits are higher than expected" and "it is assumed that the recent higher incidence of disability cases will be a permanent feature of the CPP in the years to come." However, a few months later, when an internal report by federal auditors was leaked to the press, Martin's explanation was called into question.

"The federal government knew the outlook for the Canada Pension Plan was not as grim as claimed when it issued a report early this year that the pension fund was in danger of going bankrupt," began a September 1995 article by *Toronto Star* reporter Eric Beauchesne. Two weeks before Martin announced that the plan was in crisis, Beauchesne reported, the auditors had informed him that the opposite was the case. "Over the next two to three years, we can expect a significant downward trend to be exerted on the CPP disability case load and expenditures," their memo read. "Finally," it added, "you should know that the number of applications appears to have declined significantly over the last six months." What Beauchesne—and Martin—didn't mention was that one reason disability claims had mushroomed in the previous two or three years was that some employers, during their downsizing exercises, had quietly suggested that departing employees claim company disability benefits in order to spare themselves the unpleasantness of firing them outright, or that they apply for CPP disability pensions in order to lower the costs to their employers of their severance payments.

When massive downsizing exercises in the private sector ebbed, so did the volume of disability claims. A falling-off in the claims, however, "doesn't mean that the CPP isn't struggling," Beauchesne noted, because the "aging population, for example, will continue to put pressure" on CPP finances. "That, however, has been known for years," he pointed out, "and had already been taken into account in setting schedules for premium increases." Beauchesne added tartly that the government's decision not to publicize evidence that disability payments were declining "suggests it may have been looking for justification to introduce measures to cut CPP costs." Indeed.

Since it was introduced in 1967, the Canada Pension Plan has been abused in many ways by opportunistic politicians who chose to ignore abundant and readily available evidence that Canada's unusual demographic profile would cause it to run into trouble when the vast baby-boom generation—or, at least those boomers who have not been forced into early retirement or taken it voluntarily—begins to retire in the year 2011. When the plan was brought in three decades ago, its architects knew that contribution rates would eventually have to rise, although not *how much* they would have to rise—and said so publicly.

It takes a war or an equivalent cataclysm to shift the demographic profile of a society suddenly; yet the vast majority of those who will retire in 2011, for example, were already born and living in Canada when the CPP was introduced. Although immigration, increases in longevity, or decreases in birth and fertility rates require recalculation of contribution rates from time to time, these factors are known long in advance, and are readily accommodated. The disabling maladies that have accompanied technological change—stress and repetitive strain syndrome, to name two—were less predictable, but new disabilities have been acknowledged as factors in CPP funding for years.

Politically and ideologically motivated disinformation campaigns about the finances of the plan have been common throughout its history. Indeed, Paul Martin may have learned his tactics from his Tory predecessor, Finance minister Michael Wilson, who told Canadians in December 1985 that they would soon be paying more into the Canada Pension Plan each month because the plan was "about to go broke" and needed to be fixed.

Although contribution rates must rise, Wilson said, benefits would be improved for some plan members, and the increase would guarantee the financial health of the plan for "decades to come." Moreover, the higher rates would ensure that "each generation of working Canadians" would contribute fairly to the cost of the pension benefits they will eventually receive. Without these increases, Wilson added, the plan would be "totally depleted" by the year 2003. His announcement was designed and delivered to make Canadians think that something had suddenly gone terribly wrong, and that without the contribution rate hikes, their retirement savings were at risk.

CPP contribution rates did increase on January 1, 1987, and they have been increasing each year ever since, despite the advice of Wilson's own advisory committee—outside pension experts working with the then most recent actuarial report on the plan by the federal Department of Insurance. Rate hikes were not needed until 1994, according to the committee's report, and after that, a decade of modest increases would be appropriate, to be followed by steeper increases "if necessary."

The high unemployment of the nineties—and the corporate sector's cynical abuse of CPP disability provisions as a downsizing tool—has put pressure on the plan that Wilson could not have anticipated, both by reducing contribution levels and by increasing the number of claimants. Nevertheless, the demographic profile of Canada remains the same; it is still our money; and there are many ways, short of redirecting our contributions into corporate control, to ensure that the CPP will still be in place a generation or two down the line.

When we can't trust our politicians to tell the truth about such basic matters as whether the CPP is working as it was designed to work, it is entirely understandable that so few of us trust them with our money; but do we really want an entirely privatized basic retirement-savings system? Do we want our retirement security to be at the mercy of the same global markets that have caused us such misery in this country in recent years? I think not.

Who would have thought that the Herculean battles between the Liberal government of Lester Pearson and the powerful insurance industry over the establishment of the CPP in the mid-sixties would be have to be fought all over again thirty years later in order to preserve a program whose purpose is as important today as it was then: to ensure that all working Canadians, by means of their own and their employers' contributions to the CPP, will have a subsistence income when they retire, and not become a charge upon the state. For wealthy Canadians, the Canada Pension Plan is an insignificant source of retirement income; for middle-income earners, it is the foundation of a retirement-savings plan; for low-income earners, especially women, however, it is a critical safeguard against impoverishment in later life.

The details of CPP reform were still under consideration when this book went to press, and by the time you read these words they will likely have been worked out, doubtless to no one's satisfaction. Fortunately, those who would push government right out of the retirement-savings system altogether will not have won the battle. This will be the case, in part, because saner, if equally self-interested, voices in the investment community have pointed out that to direct the entire CPP fund into private markets would create a multibillion-dollar behemoth that would in all likelihood destroy Canada's small equity and bond market. It will also be because most Rumpelstiltskins, although one would be hard-pressed to discern it in their rhetoric, *do* have a twinge of conscience when presented with images of old ladies eating cat food.

The disposition of the fund, however, is not the most important point to be made here. The point is that the corporate interests who were so determined to abolish the CPP in favour of privatizing the entire retirement-savings system have done a great disservice to Canadians. Not only have they caused many older Canadians unnecessary anxiety about the security of their retirement income, but their scare tactics have contributed greatly to younger Canadians' despair about the future.

They have been told that although there will be nothing left for them when they retire, they still must pay for the "generous" pensions of their elders. They have been told that they will face destitution in their later years unless they invest a huge chunk of their earnings in registered retirement savings plans from the day they begin to work. They have been told that all government programs are inefficient and ineffective, and that those who require them are feckless. Can it be any wonder that young Canadians are suspicious of the motives of their politicians? Should they not, however, be even more suspicious of the motives of those who are developing these messages with such insistence and so little objectivity?

It is particularly ironic that young people are being told that they must start saving for their own retirement when many of them doubt that they will ever find a job from which to retire, much less that they will ever be able to save. *Of course* it is important to save for the future, and *of course* the earlier you start to save, the faster your retirement savings will accumulate, and the less you will need to put away during your working lifetime to achieve satisfactory levels of retirement income. But would it not be more constructive for the corporate scaremongers to find ways to provide decent jobs for young Canadians, rather than terrifying them, out of sheer self-interest?

While our corporate leaders focus their energies on ways to promote self-sufficiency and boost capital accumulation in the macro-economic sphere, the micro-economic woes of young Canadians mount. The job situation for young people in Canada today is not good and, for many, it is not going to improve much in the near future. Although the unemployment rate among the young has always been higher than the national average, the gap has widened dramatically in the nineties. The recession years were devastating for young Canadians, particularly for those with high-school education or less. Between 1990 and 1995, employment opportunities for this group declined by 997,000 jobs.

More than 400,000 jobs lost during the recession were in manufacturing—a traditional provider of work for those with lower levels of education. In 1993, the manufacturing sector began to rebound, and the growth rate in factory jobs began to return to that of the late eighties. But with so many experienced older workers looking for employment, and with technology transforming the work to be done, the rebound has provided few jobs for unskilled young people. Today, according to Statistics Canada figures, more than 15 per cent of all young Canadians of working age are out of work; for those with only a high-school education or less, however, one in three is unemployed, a rate about four times that of the population as a whole, and 20 per cent higher than the average rate of other industrialized nations reported by the Organization for Economic Co-operation and Development.

Better-educated young adults are facing a different, but equally disturbing, crisis. During the recession, employment opportunities for those with postsecondary education increased by 448,000 jobs, but there are still nothing like enough jobs for even the best-educated. By mid-1996 their unemployment rate, at around 7 per cent, was significantly lower than the rate for their less-educated peers; yet thousands of highly educated young Canadians are seriously underemployed, working in part-time or other non-standard jobs, or in jobs that have little or nothing to do with their educational attainments or aspirations.

Corporate leaders and politicians tell us that the worst is now over, but caution that young people must prepare themselves for the kinds of jobs that are being created. In April 1996, Human Resources Development Canada released a comprehensive, two-volume study of where the jobs are as we approach the twenty-first century. *Jobs Future: Canada's Guide to Tomorrow's Jobs* provides as accurate a profile of the Canadian workplace for the remainder of the century as we are likely to get. It analyses the likely supply and demand for 139 different occupations in the years 1995 to 2000, detailing the education or training these jobs require and the anticipated demand for them across the country.

Jobs Future is an invaluable tool for young people attempting to tailor their education to opportunities. As a snapshot of the future, however, it makes for grim reading, especially for those without postsecondary education. Most new jobs, the report says, will be low-paying, and many will be part-time: retail salespeople, cleaners, food and beverage servers, child-care and home-support workers, kitchen workers, and clerks. But because the competition for these jobs will be high, those with minimum educational credentials will likely be out of luck.

More encouraging are the report's predictions of "significant" job opportunities for those with postsecondary education in some areas that offer higher pay and more stable employment: electrical engineering, food science, computer science, mechanical engineering, architecture, pharmacy, and civil engineering among them. These are the jobs that we used to call "skilled." In the nineties, they are called "knowledge" jobs, and all require, at the very least, an undergraduate degree.

Many of the occupations that have traditionally had the highest compensation, however, will offer young Canadians few opportunities. Law, teaching, social work, and psychology are on that list, as are sociology and dentistry. Moreover, as we have seen, many industries, such as banking, that once offered entry-level positions as an opportunity for advancement are scaling back drastically. A Deloitte & Touche study released in September 1995 predicted, for example, that 35,000 banking jobs will be lost to technology in Canada by the year 2005.

What, as parents, should we be advising our children to do in this economic climate? Obviously, we should be encouraging them to stay in school, making it clear that their chances of finding a decent job with less than a high-school education are lousy. Second, we should educate ourselves about the realities of the workplace in Canada. *Jobs Future*, the federal Department of Human Resources study cited above, which is available in any library or government bookstore, is a good place to start. Third, we should resist the temptation to trample on dreams: Life is difficult enough for young people today without our telling them that they will never find a job doing what they want to do. We will still need lawyers and doctors and teachers, albeit fewer of them, just as we will still need plumbers and automobile mechanics and computer technicians. In other words, "occupations" still exist, and will continue to exist, despite what we are told to the contrary; and we do our children a huge disservice when we suggest that they will not.

Leafing through an old sociology textbook that I must have used at some point in my educational wanderings, I was struck by how radically today's orthodoxy—the "death" of the job, the "end" of the career—differs from the received wisdom of twenty-five years ago. A section in *Sociology of Occupations and Professions* by Ronald Pavalko deals with adolescent "crises of identity," a concept that has fallen out of fashion in the nineties. The jargon may be annoying, and the words stilted, but the observations made me think that we, as a society, may be allowing an entire generation of young people to become trapped in an extended identity crisis not just by denying them jobs but also by suggesting to them that concrete plans for the future are a waste of time because "occupations" no longer exist.

"Identity crises" occur, according to the book's author, "because late adolescents and young adults do not have an occupational role which might serve as a source of personal identity and a way of locating them in the larger social structure." This "lack of occupational identity," he points out, is especially troublesome in the case of "persons who have acquired other marks of adulthood." Moreover, the consequence of "increased formal occupational preparation prior to occupational entry has been to place many persons in limbo between adolescence (a recognized and legitimate social role) and full adulthood, which normatively includes the acquisition of an occupational role and occupational identity."

A major frustration for young people today is that we are urging them to stay in school to prepare for jobs that, by and large, do not exist, in part because we, as a society, have been more interested in slashing deficits than in providing jobs for our children. At the same time, we are thoughtlessly dismissing the programs that give shape to working lives as old-fashioned nanny statism. One of the great advantages of the Canada Pension Plan, for example, is that the plan itself, if not always the uses to which governments have put our money, is easy to understand. You, as an employee, contribute to the plan, and your employer contributes an equal amount on your behalf. When you retire, you receive a benefit, indexed to inflation, for the rest of your life. This benefit is not large—in 1996, the maximum CPP pension benefit was $727.08 per month—but it will provide you with a predictable, ongoing, basic income in retirement.

Whether your basic pension is invested in capital markets or used by governments for public purposes is beside the point, so long as the benefit is guaranteed. You can, and should, augment your CPP savings throughout your working life with whatever savings you can accumulate. There is ample opportunity to invest, and the government, through the RRSP program, will give you a significant tax break for doing so. The more you save, the more you will have when you retire. Simple.

This is what we *should* be saying to our children. Instead, we announce that the CPP is "broke," and they will be too unless they can save 15 or 20 per cent of their annual income for the rest of their lives. It is gratuitously cruel to expect young people to be confident about the future while precariously balanced over a safety net that is unravelling, while their elders stand on solid ground, exhorting them to save money.

At a time when many young people are struggling to find work that will pay them enough to leave home, we really could do better than the harsh rhetoric of "self-sufficiency." Is it any wonder that so many young people operate, deliberately, in an entirely cash economy, avoiding taxes, insurance, credit—and, one might say, adulthood—convinced that it is pointless to do otherwise? Is it any wonder that they distrust government, that they see no point in voting, that they are angry and alienated, that they have lost hope in the future?

As their parents we have a lot to answer for. Many of us have been noisily defending the relentless deficit-reduction policies of our governments and voting for politicians like Mike Harris, who suggested during the 1995 Ontario election campaign that if welfare recipients found that they were unable to care for their children, they should consider giving them up. Living in one of the richest countries in the world, are we now willing to tolerate what the United Nations has identified as the second-highest rate of child poverty in the industrialized world, second only to that of the United States, the model for so many of our leaders' reforming instincts?

Perhaps it is now time to rethink our priorities, to resume the interrupted debate on better ways to organize our affairs, and our workplaces. By mid-1996, seven provinces were reporting budget surpluses, six of them for the second year in a row. This left many of their leaders scrambling to provide adequate explanations for sacrificing so many programs and causing so much hardship when a balanced budget could be achieved in such a short time. By mid-1996, the federal deficit had fallen below $30 billion, more than $3 billion ahead of Paul Martin's deficit-reduction targets. By mid-1996, Canada's short-term interest rates had dropped *below* those in the United States, with no particular effect on the value of our dollar; corporate profits were on the rise; job creation was picking up, albeit fitfully; and the Bank of Canada was fretting that its strict adherence to low-inflation targets might be pushing the economy into damaging, job-killing deflation.

In short, we can now afford to resume the critical discussions that have been postponed for so long "because there is no alternative." This does not mean, of course, the end of the corporate push to remake Canada. On the contrary, the deficit-busters are now becoming debt-busters, and will continue to invoke the same arguments and engage in the same scare tactics. Fortunately, however, it will now be much easier to spot the Rumpelstiltskins. They will be the little men jumping up and down in extreme agitation, urging us to "stay the course" until there is nothing left of Canada to save.

When the King promised the miller's daughter that her labours would soon be over and she would soon be his wife, her heart was filled with joy. But, as she stared at the room full of straw, she asked herself, How can I know that the King speaks the truth? How can I know that I shall be his wife? These were sensible questions, and the miller's daughter was wise to ask them. We would be wise to ask them too.

Chapter 5
Strong Currents of Popular Outrage

The King arrived at daybreak. When he saw the gold, he was delighted, but his heart became even more greedy. He led the miller's daughter to another, larger, room. It too was full of straw.

"If you value your life, you will spin this straw into gold before daybreak," he said, and locked her in the room.

Let us consider the straw. Was the miller so skilled in the art of persuasion that the King truly believed that straw could be spun into gold? Or did he assume that the miller intended to trick him?

When he saw that the straw had been spun into gold, did he consider that his eyes might be deceiving him? Or did he rejoice in his unaccountable good fortune?

If he was jubilant, why did he rejoice? Perhaps he wished to spread his newfound riches throughout the kingdom. But did it occur to him that if worthless straw could be spun into gold, then gold would soon be worthless? Or did he intend, on the third morning, to hide his gleaming hoard?

Did he consider that the straw might not have been spun into gold at all, but that Rumpelstiltskin had only made it seem so in order to steal his first-born child?

Let us be charitable and say that the King, in his great desire to assist his people, allowed his compassion to overwhelm his common sense.

Imagine that!

Those who would criticize the actions of global corporations must, sooner or later, consider Pat Buchanan. The combative, ultra-right-wing contender for the 1995 U.S. Republican presidential nomination campaigned on an anti-corporate platform specifically designed to appeal to Americans' fears of unemployment. Buchanan succeeded, albeit briefly, in whipping many people—and much of the media too—into a frenzy about "the greedy corporations," who, he said, were responsible for killing jobs, ripping off taxpayers, and turning their backs on the U.S. economy.

Even though he had no program for genuine corporate reform, Buchanan persuaded many Americans that his protofascist rhetoric could protect their jobs. In the process, he also convinced large numbers of Americans, many of whom already suspected as much, that immigrants were taking their jobs; that women should get out of the workplace; that gays and other minorities deserve to be bashed; that public schools subvert the morality of children; and that social-assistance programs are rewards for the lazy, the criminal, and the wicked.

It is hard to know which was more reprehensible—Buchanan's xenophobic, cynical views or his down-and-dirty tactics. In the United States, where the gulf between haves and have-nots is growing ever wider, the rush to endorse punitive solutions to every social problem has become endemic. People who have no satisfying and worthwhile work—and those who believe that their work is threatened—become bitter and enraged, and scapegoat those they hold responsible for their plight. They lash out at those they perceive to be profiting at their expense. They blame governments for being profligate with their money, and turn to politicians like Pat Buchanan, who are only too happy to exploit their fears.

Buchanan's opportunistic attack on "corporate executioners" was little more than a front for his pinched, isolationist world-view. But there are many Americans who have no sympathy with the views of xenophobic extremists, yet see what is happening to their society today as a legitimate and necessary reason to seek ways to restrain the activities of the global corporations that operate in their midst. U.S. international-development expert David Korten explains their rationale this way. "A corporate charter represents a privilege—not a right—that is extended in return for the acceptance of corresponding obligations. It is up to the people, the members of civil society—not the fictitious *persona* of the corporation—to define these privileges and obligations."

The fact that the interests of corporations and people of wealth are so tightly intertwined, Korten points out, tends to obscure the significance of the corporation in its own right. But corporations "are social inventions created to aggregate private financial resources in the service of a public purpose" and, in so far as they fail in that purpose, citizens in democratic states have always been entitled to revoke their privileges or, indeed, their charters. Less well understood, Korten says, is the tendency of corporations, as they grow in size and power, "to develop their own institutional agendas aligned with imperatives inherent in their very nature and structure that are not wholly under the control even of the people who own and manage them." These corporate agendas, which are shared by even the most socially responsible and environmentally sensitive corporate leaders, centre on increasing profits and protecting the enterprise from the uncertainties of the market.

In pursuing profits and protecting themselves from market uncertainties, however, the giant corporations that dominate the global economy are creating global havoc by throwing people out of work, destroying their environments, and destabilizing their political systems. "People in countries around the world," Korten warns, "are learning through experience that the survival of democracy itself may depend on a massive change in attitude in Western societies about the appropriate rights, privileges and powers of corporate entities."

Today, when 350 or so giant corporations are the dominant institutions of governance on the planet, Korten—and many who don't share all his views but are appalled and frightened by what they see happening in the world—are challenging corporate power by writing books and articles, organizing community groups, and imploring those who run the corporations to reconsider the wisdom and, yes, the morality of allowing quick profit to be their overriding—and, in most cases, their only—institutional objective.

That the global economy might be subject to effective democratic controls would have been dismissed by most people as utter nonsense only a decade or so ago. Technological determinism is a powerful force, and it is not easy to imagine how international markets, for example, might be regulated effectively. Yet growing numbers of thoughtful observers of Marshall McLuhan's "global village" are coming to believe not only that it is *possible* to reform postmodern capitalism, but that if massive reform is *not* undertaken soon, many countries—developing nations and prosperous industrialized nations alike—will soon face unprecedented social disruptions and environmental catastrophes, if they are not facing them already.

The "profligate consumption of non-renewable resources" is contributing to "bloody civil strife and political instability," warns Thomas Homer-Dixon, director of the peace and policy studies program at the University of Toronto and a respected authority on threats to global security. Unless the underlying causes of these scarcities are addressed, Homer-Dixon cautions, many countries will soon face a surge of violence. Increasingly, those who agree with this assessment are banding together informally and in organizations such as the People-Centered Development Forum and the Action Canada Network, which are dedicated to finding ways to make the giant multinationals more accountable for the human and ecological consequences of their activities, and to persuade or oblige them to put the technology transforming workplaces around the world to uses that will benefit everyone, not just an élite few.

Their ideas, many of them in the formative stages but some (such as the "Tobin tax" on foreign exchange transactions) more fully developed, provide a glimmer of hope that the forces destabilizing local economies—which have deprived as many as fifty million people of their jobs in the twenty-five industrialized OECD countries alone—will one day soon be deployed more equitably and more humanely. (The Tobin tax is a proposal made by the 1981 Nobel prize winner in economics, James Tobin, that a levy in the order of .05 percent be collected on all spot foreign exchange transactions in order to dampen speculative international financial movements. The tax would be too small to deter commodity trades or serious investment commitments, but would oblige investors to focus on the long term, thereby giving greater autonomy to individual coutries. The tax could be used, Tobin suggested, to finance the operations of the United Nations and its agencies, and to establish a debt repayment fund to help developing counties retire their international debts, enabling them to climb out of the debt holes into which they were lured by global lenders seeking profit. The objectives of the critics of the multinational corporations defy the pessimistic predictions of many experts. "The dominant world economic system— Capitalism Triumphant—is failing to provide food, shelter, clothing, education and health care which the poorer people of the world want and need but are not in a position to demand," observed British sociologist Peter Senker two years ago, in a typically gloomy assessment of the "inevitable" social consequences of globalization. In Senker's view, expressed in a 1995 article entitled "Technological Change and the Future of Work," "economic development around the world is dominated, and seems likely to continue to be dominated for the foreseeable future by the production and development of products, services and materials which meet the needs only of the affluent."

Many of those who are looking for ways to ensure that this will not be the case are considerably more optimistic than Senker. Much of their optimism springs from their knowledge that the way entire societies perceive reality can shift very quickly. William Sullivan, an American philosopher whose primary interest is in the tensions between democracy and globalization, for example, observes that politics in the United States "may be at the beginning of a sea-change, a moment of serious challenge to the twenty-year-long ascendancy of the neo-capitalist creed that the market should determine both the worth and the destiny of persons and communities."

A turning-point may now have been reached, Sullivan observes in "The Politics of Meaning as a Challenge to Neocapitalism," in the May/June 1996 issue of *Tikkun*, "analogous to the great shift a century ago from the brutal *laissez-faire* of the Gilded Age to the reforming era of Progressivism." In his view, and in that of many others, "strong currents of outrage are swelling against what many perceive as the amoral destructiveness of uncontrolled market forces gone global."

In May 1996, economists, development experts, consumer advocates, and environmentalists from around the world gathered in Washington, D.C., at the second International Forum on Globalization to discuss how to identify and promote a "third way" between the needs and aspirations of large multinational corporations and the narrow, backwards-looking protectionism advocated by economic nationalists. Their goals were stunningly ambitious:

to find ways to return control of investment to national governments; to find ways to protect the global environment by encouraging genuinely sustainable development; and to find ways to maintain local businesses threatened by the global economy.

The forum followed hard on the heels of February's G-7 jobs summit in Lille, France, where French president Jacques Chirac argued that Europe, which is in the grip of massive unemployment, should be seeking a "third path" between free-wheeling U.S.–style capitalism and the more highly regulated European economic environment. Chirac's comments did not sit well with hard-core defenders of unfettered markets and their media cheerleaders.

Shortly after the French president made his remarks, for example, *Globe and Mail* columnist Terence Corcoran, a determined defender of the sanctity of market forces, took issue with them in a classic, if by now rather tired, restatement of the corporate credo: "The cause of Europe's unemployment crisis has been identified in numerous studies" by the Organization for Economic Co-operation and Development, Corcoran wrote, "as a function of too much government, pro-union labour laws, protectionist trade policies and overgenerous welfare systems. Extreme environmental regulations are also a factor, along with tax rates that destroy incentives and heavy debt loads that reduce investment."

Corcoran continued with an observation that must have baffled his Canadian readers. "In North America," he wrote, "job growth has been spectacular, relatively, thanks mostly to freer labour markets, fewer government financed employment and unemployment schemes, and lower tax rates in the United States." Chirac's "third way, down the middle between Europe and the United States, would be Canada," he added, "where the middle has invariably produced middling results."

Noting, finally, that job growth in Canada has not kept pace with that of the United States, where official unemployment rates are among the lowest in the industrial world, Corcoran concluded his column with the sarcastic comment: "Leave it to the Europeans to decide that, between a system that works and one that doesn't, the route to take is the one that almost works some of the time."

Well, maybe. Later in this chapter, we will examine just how well the U.S. system "works" for millions of its citizens, including a further 10 per cent or so who are "unofficially" unemployed. But, for now, let's just say that those who are committed to finding ways to temper the most blatant abuses of unbridled global enterprise can take some comfort in the fact that many Americans who enthusiastically applauded the emergence of the global economy are now expressing serious reservations about its long-term viability unless its excesses are curbed. To be sure, these reservations are to some extent a case of what goes around comes around. Indeed, many of their concerns are strikingly similar to those Paul Hellyer raised twenty years ago, when he cautioned Canadians that capitalism, as practised in the late twentieth century, would steal their jobs and alter their peaceable kingdom forever. But there is also a new message: that the global economy may be in danger of self-destructing.

When such opinions are voiced by people who have embraced "globalization" as the best hope for a troubled world, it is time for the rest of us to listen up. "Nearly everyone applauds today's complex web of global trade, production, and finance as the highest stage of capitalism," wrote Benjamin Schwarz, in "Why America Thinks It Has to Run the World," published in the June 1996 issue of the conservative-leaning *Atlantic Monthly*. "But international capitalism may be approaching a crisis just as it is reaching its fullest flower."

A genuinely interdependent world market, Schwarz cautions, is "extraordinarily fragile." The emergent high-technology industries are "the most powerful engines of world economic growth," but they require "a level of specialization and a breadth of markets that are possible only in a completely integrated global economy." That integrated economy, so far as it exists at all, Schwarz warns, is in imminent danger of collapse. Inequities in employment and in the distribution of wealth are causing many countries to turn inward, in increasingly desperate attempts to ward off social unrest and political turmoil.

This assessment is echoed by William Bridges. The de-jobbed world that is emerging is not without its "severe societal and psychological dangers," Bridges warns in *Job Shift*, adding: "I have some serious misgivings about de-jobbing and about what a future shaped by it is going to be like. I worry a good deal about that, not because I think that people (including the poor) cannot make a go of it, but because it represents such a huge change that I am afraid we will rip ourselves apart making the transition to get from here to there." Social reaction and political fanaticism thrive during times of transition, Bridges cautions, "and we can already see signs of increasing xenophobia and isolationism in all the industrialized countries."

Schwarz, a senior fellow at the World Policy Institute in New York City, argues that the United States must bear much of the blame for the increasing fragility of the world economy. U.S. foreign policy during the Cold War, he says, was designed to build and maintain "an international economic order" as much as, if not more than, it was designed to contain communism. These policies were so successful, he observes, that although the Cold War has ended, the United States must continue to pursue virtually identical policies in order to maintain the global economy it created so deliberately.

However, that economy is in danger of breaking down, Schwarz warns, because the United States, having created it, seems now to be losing control. "Lenin argued seventy-eight years ago that international capitalism would be economically successful but, by growing in a world of competitive states, would plant the seeds of its own destruction," Schwarz notes. The greatest irony today, he adds, is that "the worldwide economic system that the United States fostered has itself largely determined America's relative decline even as it has contributed to the country's economic growth. Through trade, foreign investment, and the spread of technology and managerial expertise, economic power has diffused from the United States to new centers of growth, thus undermining American hegemony and ultimately jeopardizing the world economy."

Many Americans' vague perceptions that their own jobs are now threatened by the consequences of the economic imperialism that was once their greatest hope for continued prosperity play into the hands of economic nationalists such as Pat Buchanan, whose xenophobic views seemed to offer a return to happier times. However, its marked similarities to Hitler's appeals to disaffected, unemployed Germans in the thirties deeply frightened more thoughtful Americans. Now, with Buchanan's inward-looking economic nationalism lurking as a constant undercurrent in U.S. politics, many of them are determined to find solutions to the daunting problems associated with the global economy before they lead to rhetoric even more violent than Buchanan's.

When protectionist urges surface in the United States, as they have done with increasing frequency in recent trade disputes, they send a chill down the spine of America's trading partners, including Canada. In May 1996, for example, federal Trade minister Arthur Eggleton lashed out at American trade officials for their unwillingness to negotiate rules under the free-trade agreement with Canada that would blunt the growing threat of protectionist U.S. measures against alleged subsidies and dumping. American protectionism, Eggleton said at the time, was "pointing towards a beggar-my-neighbour approach" that will force other countries to react in the same vein. "Protectionism breeds protectionism," Eggleton warned, echoing Schwarz's cautions.

When Americans begin to doubt that the global economy is working for them, Canadians would do well to examine what has gone wrong, in the fervent hope that, as we
pursue the global dream, we can find ways to avoid the
divisions that are ripping that society apart. What does it
mean to say that American society is divided? It means,
among other things, that more than five million Americans
are in jail, or under the supervision of the courts. It means
that "gated" housing developments with private security
forces and barb-wired walls are mushrooming across the
country. It means that the real incomes of most Americans
have been falling for more than twenty years, while the
incomes of the very wealthiest Americans have grown out
of all proportion. It means that growing numbers of
Americans have no medical insurance and no way to pay
for medical services. It means Oklahoma City, and local
militias, and torched black churches. It means, in short, living in a society that is increasingly consumed by fear.

Against their most deeply ingrained free-enterprise
beliefs, many Americans on the right of the political spectrum are beginning to suspect that the root cause of these
social cataclysms is what the conservative American historian Edward Luttwak has called "turbo-charged capitalism,"
which condemns those without marketable skills to a lifetime of declining earnings and declining expectations. The
new economy, Luttwak says, has eliminated many of the
low-paid but respectable jobs that once allowed a striving
section of the U.S. underclass to rise into the working class.

This is a phenomenon that is well understood. But
Luttwak goes further, pointing out that the upheavals and
disruptions of the new economy condemn most working
Americans of *all* skill levels to lives of chronic economic
insecurity. "As entire industries rise and fall much faster
than before, as firms expand, shrink, merge, downsize, and
restructure at an unprecedented pace," he observes, "their
employees at all but the highest levels must go to work
each day without knowing whether they will still have

their job the next."

That the less-skilled "are becoming further impoverished merely means that the country's well documented unequal distribution of wealth will continue," Luttwak points out, but the consequences of the acute economic insecurities of the middle-class majority are potentially even more explosive. "The underclass (less than 5 percent of the U.S. population) can only retaliate by individual criminality, with occasional mini-pogroms against the privileged"; the working poor "silently accept their lot and even feel guilty about it, but no society can fail to pay a heavy price for widespread middle-class insecurity." One doesn't have to be a historian of pre–Second World War Europe, Luttwak adds, to recognize the connection between what the economy is doing to most Americans and the increasingly intolerant climate of contemporary American life.

"Visitors to the United States nowadays often point out that more and more things are legally or socially prohibited in the Land of the Free," Luttwak continues, "because the insecure majority does not realize that the economy too can be subject to the will of the majority (it believes in Invisible Hands, in the unchallengeable sovereignty of the market, and in the primacy of economic efficiency, so it vents its anger and resentment by punishing, restricting, and prohibiting everything it can.)" For if there is one thing Americans still want their governments to do for them, it is to protect them from criminals. The most blatant symptom of these punitive tendencies, Luttwak points out, is "the insatiable demand for tougher criminal laws, longer prison sentences, mandatory life sentences for repeat offenders, more and prompter executions, and harsher forms of detention (including, of late, chain gangs.)"

One way to look at all these trends is to see them as the American credo of individualism hitting the wall of global competition, in which jobs can disappear overnight. The tendency to glorify individualism at the expense of community has long distinguished the American mind-set from

Canadians' more community-oriented approach to social problems, and when incomes and expectations were on the rise in both countries, both models worked tolerably well.

Now, however, as expectations are on the decline and the chasm between the well-off and the poor in the United States is widening, the focus on individual rights is exacerbating, not relieving, social tensions. "The big story of the era of conservative rule" in the United States, Stanford economist Paul Krugman observes in his 1994 book, *Peddling Prosperity: Economic Sense and Nonsense in the Age of Diminishing Expectations*, "was not the growth of income, but its distribution. Once you correct for the ups and downs of the business cycle, the growth path of the economy was virtually the same before and after Ronald Reagan took office. But the conservative era was marked by a huge fanning out of the spread of incomes, with the rich becoming far richer, the poor a lot poorer, and the middle class going nowhere in particular."

In a country where any constraints on the freedom of individuals or of corporations have traditionally been considered to be philosophically unacceptable—even if those limitations are in the interests of society as a whole—hard economic times for the many are creating major and unwelcome disruptions in the lives of the comfortable few. Not only do many Americans live in constant fear of crime, they are also retreating into the dark caves of intolerance, xenophobia, and narrow self-interest.

Above all, they have come to distrust government, which, because it exists to protect and advance collective interests, is seen to be threatening them personally. As a result, they have voted in politicians committed to dismantling the laws and regulations put into place to curb the socially harmful activities of individuals and corporations. Social programs designed to help the poor and the unemployed have been abandoned on the grounds that they interfere with the operations of the free market. Public services have been privatized on the grounds that they could operate more efficiently as money-making ventures. At the same time, corporate taxes have been cut, on the grounds that it is government's job to further corporate enterprise, not protect the public interest.

Terence Corcoran is correct when he points out that the U.S. economy is a powerful generator of jobs: The official unemployment rate in the United States in mid-1996 was about 5.6 per cent. But he might also have pointed out, when criticising Jacques Chirac's quest for a "third path" between the American way and the European way, that in the land of opportunity the income of nearly eighty million Americans is lower today that it was twenty years ago. According to the U.S. Bureau of Labor Statistics, one of the effects of the massive restructuring of the last two decades is that average real wages are roughly 9 per cent below what they were in 1975. If this trend continues, Edward Luttwak observes, the United States will fit virtually every definition of a third-world country by the year 2020.

Corcoran might also have noted that of the millions of new jobs created in the United States in the nineties, by far the greatest number are low-skill service jobs with low pay, few benefits, and no security. He might have pointed out that temporary, contract, and part-time workers now make up more than 25 per cent of the U.S. workforce, a percentage that is expected to rise rapidly in the coming years. (The U.S. National Planning Association has estimated that by the turn of the century, more than 35 per cent of the U.S. workforce will be "contingent" workers.) These are the people Jeremy Rifkin referred to as "the new reserve army," those whose labour "can be used and discarded at a moment's notice and at a fraction of the cost" of maintaining a permanent workforce.

The implications of these massive trends are only now beginning to be understood fully. Part-time temporary workers in the United States earn, on average, 20 to 40 per cent less than full-time workers doing comparable work. Moreover, while about 88 per cent of full-time workers

have some form of health insurance through their employers, fewer than 25 per cent of temporary workers have any
health insurance at all. Similarly, while about 50 per cent of
full-time workers are covered by employee pension plans,
only about 15 per cent of part-time workers can look forward to pension benefits of any kind.

Much of this inequality, Rifkin points out, is the result of
deliberate corporate policy of the last two decades. Chris
Tilly of the Policy and Planning Institute at the University of
Massachusetts, for example, found that at least 42 per cent
of the growth in inequality of wages and income in the
United States is directly attributable to management decisions "to create a two-tier labor force of well-paid core
workers and poorly-paid contingent workers."

Their actions, Rifkin says, are "killing the American
Dream" that "propelled generations of immigrants to work
hard in the belief that they could better their lot in life and
improve the prospects for their children." In its place, he
warns, is "a growing cynicism about corporate power and
increased suspicion of the men and women who wield near
total control over the global marketplace." Most Americans,
he adds, "feel trapped by the new lean-production practices
and sophisticated new automation technologies, not knowing if or when the re-engineering drive will reach into their
own office or workstation, plucking them from what they
once thought was a secure job and casting them into the
reserve army of contingent workers, or worse yet, the
unemployment line."

The unquestioning belief in the efficacy of an unregulated market system makes those who tell us that Canada's
only hope is to become more like the United States oblivi-
ous to what is actually happening in U.S. workplaces. For
Terence Corcoran, for example, to extol low U.S. unemployment rates without even considering the price paid by
Americans—in falling expectations, falling wages, and
social disruption—to achieve them, and the price yet to be
paid—in terms of instability and incivility—if nothing is

done to narrow the income gap is wilful blindness. The same refusal on the part of free-market zealots to acknowledge the dangers of limiting the ability of government to moderate the abuses of market forces is provoking outrage around the world. It is also convincing a great many people that the survival of democracy may be at stake and that we must find ways to reverse the trend towards less government that has driven neoconservative policies in the last twenty years.

As David Korten has pointed out, many of these policies have been self-defeating anyway, in that they have increased the fragility, not the strength, of the global economy. Although opposed to deficit spending, the Reagan administration, he observes, made many decisions that weakened the United States' economic position in the world. By eschewing government control in economic planning and priority setting, the Reaganite neoconservatives left the future of the United States entirely in the hands of corporations being pressed by capital markets to focus on short-term profits, not on long-term planning and development; and by allowing corporations to pursue deliberate anti-labour policies, they "squandered the United States' key resource in the global marketplace—its human capital."

The results of these decisions—combined with massive military spending that contributed to making the United States the world's leading deficit spender—Korten observes, was an overall weakening of U.S. economic strength compared with that of Japan and Western Europe, with far-reaching, "clearly harmful" consequences to ordinary citizens. In the end, he adds, they may turn out to have been fatally harmful to many corporations as well.

These corporate policies were not the result of a conspiracy, Korten is at pains to point out. "Major shifts in national policy do not come about as a consequence of corporate and political elites gathering in a conference room to define a strategy for imposing global adjustment."

American entrepreneurs, he notes, are far too independent minded and represent too broad a range of conflicting interests for that. Rather the policies were the result of what Walden Bello, in his 1994 book, *Dark Victory: The United States, Structural Adjustment, and Global Poverty*, called "the ascendance of an ideology, a set of theories, beliefs and myths with some internal coherence" that came to be seen by many Americans—especially those whose interests the ideology furthered—as both necessary and inevitable. "Transmitted through universities, corporations, churches and political parties," Bello points out, the ideology eventually comes to be internalized by large numbers of people, especially those whose interests it principally expresses, but also by those who have little or no access to alternative ideas.

This account of how a set of ideas takes hold is not a bad description of how the ideology surrounding deficit reduction in Canada came to be pervasive. With such organizations as the right-wing National Citizens' Coalition, with its ample resources and anonymous corporate membership, the Canadian Bankers Association, and the ultra-conservative Business Council on National Issues leading the parade, the mainstream press quickly jumped on the rapid-deficit-reduction bandwagon, as did politicians elected on promises of job creation. With the Rae government in Ontario and the Chrétien government federally caving in to corporate pressure—and with right-wing economists such as the Fraser Institute's Michael Walker shouting down all dissenters—what choice did we see but to buy into the mind-set?

Nor is it a bad description of how many people who stand to lose from economic policies that serve only the interests of corporations and the wealthy come to believe in them nonetheless. When an idea is in the air—especially an idea like the evils of deficit spending, with its overtones of impending societal cataclysm—it can overwhelm all alternatives and all dissenting voices. Sometimes it can overwhelm the evidence too.

One reason so many Canadians became obsessed with government deficits in the early nineties—even those who lost important services and programs and, in some cases, their jobs—may be because the concept of government debt translates so readily into the language of ordinary household economies. That government deficits bear little relationship to personal deficits—to the unsecured debts we run up on our credit cards, for example—is not easy to explain in the space or time typically available to those who would disagree with the prevailing orthodoxy in op-ed pieces or in the television and radio interviews that are our primary sources of information on these matters.

Canadians were staggering under record levels of personal debt even *before* they started losing their jobs during the recession. The pressure of their own debts made them sitting ducks for those who told them that there is no difference between government deficits and their own maxed-out Visa cards. It often seemed as if the media were suckers for the analogy too; perhaps because it provided a simple—or simplistic—explanation of complex issues.

We all understand, even though we don't necessarily act according to our understanding, that it is not good to get into debt beyond our ability to repay. Mortgages are okay, because they are attached to—or *used to* be attached to— property that will increase in value over time. Borrowing to buy a car is okay too, because we need a car to get to work, where we earn—or *used to* earn—the money to pay for it. Borrowing money to contribute to our RRSPs is also okay, because the contribution gives us a tax break and the money we borrow will grow, tax-deferred, over time, if we invest it wisely—or luckily. Borrowing money to buy disposable goods or to support lavish lifestyles, however, is definitely not okay, unless we have sufficient money coming in to repay the debt before interest accrues.

This is the economy of personal deficit spending. But government deficits are different. In part, they represent an investment in the future, just as, in part, they provide the means for an economy to *create* wealth. As economists of every political stripe would agree, this distinction is well understood in the private sector. Corporations distinguish between the portion of their debt created by current spending and the portion dedicated to creating future profits. But most of us have accepted without question that *all* government deficits must be reduced to zero, no matter the cost to social programs, no matter the cost to Canada as we know it.

As a result, many of us have accepted the proposition that it is downright wicked for our governments to borrow to invest in education, or in research and development, or in retraining, or in any other programs whose benefits will come to fruition only in the future. Many of us have also accepted the illogical proposition that deficits are the underlying cause of unemployment, rather than its symptom.

Yet, when a high proportion of a country's population is unemployed, inevitably several things follow that are no more difficult to understand than the notion that it is foolish to borrow money to buy fripperies. First, those without work or who are underemployed are unable to contribute to the economy's productive potential, and their skills and talents are wasted. Second, those without work do not pay taxes, and government revenues are reduced. Third, large numbers of those without work require some form of state assistance to get by, and this further depletes public coffers.

These depletions lead, in turn, to unanticipated crises in government-sponsored programs, such as the Canada Pension Plan. When fewer people are working, fewer people are contributing to the plan. As well, more people are drawing money from the plan, forced to claim their benefits early because they have no work and few prospects of finding work. These shortfalls, in turn, make it necessary that contribution rates rise, adding to the tax burden of all those who are fortunate enough to have jobs, and of their employers. Our politicians and corporate leaders, however, blame the woes of the CPP on the demographic trends that were provided for in the plan a long time ago. It is unemployment that has created the current CPP crisis, and it is unemployment, not demography, that is the primary threat to our children's future in the nineties.

Many of today's workplace trends, virtually all of them instigated by large corporate employers trying to please their shareholders by increasing their short-term profits, have had more subtle effects on Canada's employment system as well. Today, about two million Canadians are self-employed, a trend that was well under way before the recession propelled many more people who would have preferred to keep their jobs into self-employment. According to Statistics Canada, the number of self-employed Canadians grew by 56,000 between 1990 and 1992, when 385,000 Canadians lost their jobs. During the downsizing frenzy that came hard on the heels of the recession, the ranks of the self-employed grew by a staggering 171,000, a gain of 9.4 per cent. (Hiring, by comparison, increased by only 2.3 per cent.)

On the face of it, this seems like good news. Entrepreneurial activity is traditionally a reliable indicator of a nation's economic health, and many people find self-employment both liberating and profitable. However, many of these people were *forced* into self-employment when their employers decided to contract out or eliminate their jobs in an effort to increase their profits by reducing their costs. In some cases, as we have seen, ex-employees found themselves doing virtually the same work they had done before, but for less money and no benefits.

The personal losses incurred in such situations are clearly devastating, but the losses to government revenues, and therefore to society as a whole, can be equally damaging. Farewell to employer contributions to the Canada Pension Plan. Farewell to unemployment-insurance contributions. Farewell to disability and extended health-care and life insurance, to which employers may have contributed.

Farewell to employer-sponsored pension plans. Farewell to the old social contract, and with it a great many of employers' traditional responsibilities.

Contracting-out, as we have seen, weakens the employment system in another way, too. Contract workers make up some of their losses because their self-employed status entitles them to deductions that may lower their income taxes. This is a soupçon of good news for them, but it is bad news for government revenues. In effect, contracting-out allows large corporations to breach an understanding with Canadians that has stood us in good stead for half a century: that employers have an obligation to contribute to the future well-being of their employees as a part of doing business in Canada.

When we look at our current difficulties in light of such facts as these, it seems transparently obvious that our politicians should be focusing their energies on getting people back to work—and on persuading the corporate community that they should not abandon their traditional responsibilities, if only because it is not in their long-term interest to do so. (The flood of new studies and books on "corporate anorexia"—a company's loss of effectiveness due to excessive shrinkage—should convince them, even if governments can't.)

It is also obvious that even as they were demanding that governments slash their deficits, corporate employers were both driving up these public deficits and pressuring politicians to gut public services and social programs to control them. The terrible irony is, however, that many of us don't want our governments to make efforts to constrain the corporations on our behalf. For in accepting the corporate argument that deficits must be wrestled to the ground before we can focus on job creation, we have also accepted the corporate credo that no government can be trusted to spend our tax dollars wisely, or to protect our best interests.

This lack of trust has led us, in turn, to allow conservative politicians such as Ralph Klein in Alberta and Mike

Harris in Ontario to accede to the demands of the private sector that governments at all levels should be radically downsized, as Harris puts it, "for the sake of our children in the future." Is it not at least possible that this is short-sighted folly, rather than good common sense? Is it not at least possible that he is dead wrong?

Is it not at least possible that Canada's drift towards creating the American-style workplaces that multinational corporations demand—workplaces in which a small élite enjoys jobs with high pay, benefits programs, pension plans, and a measure of job security, while the rest of us, if we can find jobs at all, will work for low pay, no benefits, no pension plans, and no job security—is not in our best interest as a society? This outcome, surely, is not what most of us want. Yet it is the logical consequence of the decisions so many of us have made to vote for politicians so committed to getting government off the backs of the corporations that they are willing to take measures—measures unthinkable only a few years ago—that will diminish our lives, and the very nature of our society, forever.

Perhaps it is not surprising that the King, wishing to help his people, persuaded himself that worthless straw could indeed be spun into gold. Nor, perhaps, is it surprising that the miller's daughter, left alone in a locked room and assigned an impossible task, was willing to promise Rumpelstiltskin anything, including her first-born child, to save her own life. She was frightened; and her father, knowing that she could not spin straw into gold, had betrayed her.

Chapter 6
Global Warriors Meet Working Women in Cyberspace

The miller's daughter looked around the huge room stuffed with straw. Not even the little man, she thought, could help her this time.

But where, you may wish to know, was the miller's wife as these extraordinary events unfolded? Was she dead? If she was living, did she not wonder, for three long nights, where her daughter might be?

Did she know that her husband had persuaded the King that their daughter knew how to spin straw into gold?

If she knew, did she hurry to the King to plead for her daughter's life? Did she beg her husband to confess that he knew his daughter had no notion of how to spin straw into gold?

Let us say that the miller's wife was a patient, trusting woman. Let us say also that she was familiar with her husband's ambition and pride, yet chose to trust him nonetheless.

But did she share his conviction that the poor of the kingdom lived in poverty because they were not so clever as he was, he who had persuaded the King that his daughter could spin straw into

gold? Or did she think him a fool, whose schemes would never suc-
ceed, though he risked his daughter's life to further them?

If she knew that her daughter's life was in peril, why did the
miller's wife do nothing?

In April 1996, *The Economist*, the British-based magazine
that chronicles the transactions of the global economy, ran
a story headlined "Sexual Speculations." In the United
States, the unsigned piece noted, the recent voting patterns
of men and women in presidential elections appear to
reflect differing perceptions of the great neoconservative
mission to free private enterprise from government constraints so that Americans may prosper in the new world
economy. Beginning with the election of Democrat Jimmy
Carter in 1976, the article observed, a persistent gap has
appeared, with Democrats faring much better in presidential voting among women than among men.

Women *did* vote for the global warrior Ronald Reagan
over the community-oriented Carter by 47 versus 46 per
cent in 1980; but, among men, the divide, at 55 per cent
for Reagan and 38 per cent for Carter, was much wider. In
1992, Bill Clinton won the women's vote against George
Bush by a substantial 45 versus 37 per cent, while, among
men, the split was quite narrow, at 41 versus 38 per cent.
Then, in April 1996, a *Time*/Yankelovich/CNN poll showed
that the gap between women and men was growing.
Women's support for Clinton was running at nearly 60 per
cent, while only 48 per cent of men said that they preferred
the incumbent to his challenger, Bob Dole, the old-
fashioned Republican moderate who had defeated Pat
Buchanan for the Republican nomination.

Women don't vote as a bloc, the article noted, and race
and education remain more important than gender as pre-
dictors of party preference in the United States. Still, these
persistent voting gaps suggest that, in general, men are
more inclined than women to vote for candidates who say
that they will drastically reduce government's role in the

operations of the market economy and in the delivery of social programs. The significant change in voting patterns in the past twenty years, *The Economist* observed, was not that more women voted for Democrats, but that men were stampeding into Republican ranks.

In the seventies the explanation for the difference seemed to be "women's greater distaste for the use of force, whether it was used to combat crime at home or communists abroad," the article noted. But in the nineties, men seem much more inclined than women to want government "to get out of the way" of business. Women, or at least the women who vote in presidential elections, are inclined to see government as a buffer *against* the new economy, and want Washington more, not less, involved in overseeing and regulating the marketplace and in providing and overseeing social programs, health care, and education.

For many reasons it is impossible to take a comparable snapshot of men's and women's voting patterns in recent Canadian federal elections. For one thing, the multiparty parliamentary system precludes a simple count along gender lines. For another, when they elected the Chrétien Liberals in 1993, many Canadians—men and women alike—believed that they *were* voting for a party dedicated to preserving the country's social programs and creating jobs. Similarly, many Ontarians, when they elected Bob Rae's New Democrats in 1990, believed that they were electing a government that would challenge corporate orthodoxy. And although at the provincial level the victories of the ultra-conservative, program-slashing governments of Ralph Klein in Alberta in 1993 and Mike Harris in Ontario in 1995 might seem to run counter to a gender trend, support for these governments plummeted among women when the far-reaching implications of their drastic cuts to education and social programs became apparent.

Although gender differences in our perceptions of the appropriate role of government in a democratic society obviously are tricky to analyse, public-opinion polls—and massive demonstrations against government cut-backs organized by women's groups in Ottawa, Toronto, Quebec City, and elsewhere—suggest that in Canada, as in the United States, women are not persuaded that the benefits of radically reducing the role of government in our lives outweigh the perils of so doing. Women are also inclined to be somewhat sceptical about the benefits of the technology that drives the global economy, and it is not hard to understand why. New technology has always been controlled by men, so it can hardly be surprising that women might feel suspicious of—and excluded from—the decision-making processes that determine how and when it will be deployed, and at whose expense.

Women feel excluded because, by and large, they *are* excluded. A 1995 study, conducted by Leo-Paul Lauzon, a professor of accounting at the University of Quebec in Montreal, for example, found that women are conspicuous by their absence at the highest corporate levels. Lauzon studied the 1992 annual reports of 776 Canadian companies, including Power Corp., Teleglobe Canada Ltd., and the Oshawa Group, and found that women made up only 5.5 per cent of board members and 7.5 per cent of company officers. He also learned that 57.5 per cent of publicly traded companies had no female directors at all, while 52.2 per cent had not one woman in their top executive ranks.

Furthermore, Lauzon discovered, the larger the corporation, the less likely are women to be found at the very top levels of management. His study indicated, for example, that women made up only 4.5 per cent of officers in the Canadian companies that report more than $1 billion in equity. They were somewhat better represented in companies with equity between $20 million and $50 million, but still comprised only about 10 per cent of top managers. The financial-services sector, with just 9 per cent female officers and 8 per cent female directors, was most welcoming to women, but their representation at the top bears little relationship to the numbers of women these institutions employ.

It has been my experience that women are not at all frightened by technology. Technology makes our day-to-day lives more manageable, just as it sometimes makes them more enjoyable. Large numbers of us would be lost without our computers and our fax machines, just as many of us can wander in cyberspace as freely and as confidently as most men. Many of us, however, *are* frightened by the uses to which technology may be put in the tunnel-visioned corporate quest to improve short-term profits.

When technology costs us our jobs or makes them less interesting, or closes doors that once were open to us, we wonder if it *has* to be this way, and we recall some of the truly spectacular mistakes corporate strategists have made in recent years by committing to costly new systems that swiftly became obsolete or simply didn't work very well. "On-line systems are brittle," observes Clifford Stoll, in his 1995 critique of the information highway, *Silicon Snake Oil*. "They work when everything's normal, but are exquisitely sensitive to software, hardware, and communications problems. A stream of data can't wait for the computer—if it's not decoded immediately, bits fall onto the floor." This is why, Stoll notes, there are so many reports of commodity-exchange programs "that pass all their tests, yet fail just when the computers slow down from a heavy load."

Moreover, Stoll points out, even systems that work can prove to be costly mistakes. The value of a new computer, for example, drops by half within two years, and within five years the computer itself will have become obsolete. Word-processing software lasts about two years before it is superseded; but ironically, new software programs run more slowly than the ones they replace.

When we see men swooning over expensive new systems with fabulous functionalities, we wonder whether they might be making a mistake when they decide to invest millions of dollars—dollars that would pay quite a few salaries for quite a few years—in technology that may not live up to their expectations, or may be too powerful for the job, or will be so hated by the people who must use it that they manage never to quite master it. We marvel at their conviction that the more work technology can do for us, the better off we all will be, just as we shake our heads at their naïve belief that all new technologies will work like charms and spin profits as efficiently as Rumpelstiltskin seemed to turn the King's straw into gold. Men, according to studies of "early adopters"—those who like new technology simply because it is new—are easily persuaded that the shinier the machine, the better it will work and the more likely it will be to outperform human beings. Women, on the other hand, need to be convinced not only that the new technology will work, but also that it will work better than the systems we happen to be using. If our spinning-wheels work just fine, we are inclined to be suspicious of Rumpelstiltskins bearing pricy new wheels apparently able to spin straw into gold.

We become even more suspicious when the corporate quest for short-term profit through technology-driven efficiencies is undertaken in the context of an ideology that wishes to remake society in ways that strike us as demonstrably foolish and misguided—and that seem likely to work to our disadvantage, and to the disadvantage of our children.

As computer technology has displaced workers in the nineties, we observe unemployment and widespread fear of job loss have marginalized workplace-equity initiatives. Take, as one example, the ongoing attack in Canada on daycare and early childhood education, a joint initiative undertaken by U.S.–style global warriors—who view the allocation of public moneys for child-care programs as too expensive—and backward-looking fundamentalist scolds—who view daycare for the children of working mothers as morally wrong. We are inclined to think that those who agree with Ontario premier Mike Harris that women, if they insist on working, ought to leave their children with a relative or pay a neighbour to look after them, or, *in extremis*, give them up, have rocks in their heads and malice in their hearts.

The social-Darwinist tendencies of the ultra-conservative social ideology is baldly exposed in highly political efforts to discredit daycare and the women who rely on it. Apparently inspired by the vitriolic rhetoric of loopy U.S. Christian fundamentalists, Canadian anti-day-care zealots want nothing less than to undo the progress of the last two or three decades in ensuring that our children are safe, happy, and engaged for those hours when they are in the care of others. Fronted by a Calgary-based group called the National Foundation for Family Research and Education, founded by the controversial psychologist Mark Genuis, the anti-daycare movement is noisily promoted by survival-of-the-fittest crusaders such as *Financial Post* columnist and aspiring leader of the reactionary right, David Frum; his neoconservative chum, *Saturday Night* editor Kenneth Whyte; and, now that they have thrown Jan Brown out, the entire Reform Party caucus.

Frum's wife, Danielle Crittenden, a working mother of two, added her voice to the chorus in an article in the April 1996 edition of *Saturday Night* entitled "The Mother of All Problems," and touted on the magazine's cover as "The Madness of Working Women." In it, Crittenden argues that mothers who work are gripped by guilt and frustration. "It's strange," she says, "that in all the public discussions of the problems faced by working mothers, the most animating aspect of motherhood—that we love our children and want to be with them as much as possible—goes unmentioned."

This is not because everyone takes this fact for granted, she continues, but because "if you believe even modestly in women's equality, it is a fact that is too frightening to confront." The tension "created by the denial of this fact," Crittenden adds, "is felt by every working mother at nearly every moment of her working day. It grips her round her leg when she leaves in the morning and hurls itself at her when she come back through the door each evening."

Well, maybe. Crittenden's emotional outburst says a great deal about her and the financially comfortable women she profiles in the article—one of whom, the vice-president of a bank, ought to go home forthwith to her new kitchen "the size of a small urban park" and stay there, given the burden of guilt she piles on herself each day by working. But Crittenden's attempt to generalize her argument to *all* working mothers is a sham. Even more worrisome is that disinformation campaigns of this sort take on a life of their own, especially among those inclined to see daycare as a plot against free enterprise. The contempt of the anti-daycare crowd for those who have struggled to ensure that their children receive the best care possible while their parents are at work is mirrored in angry letters-to-the-editor from Cold Warriors unwilling to concede that it is pointless to continue the war against a vanquished enemy.

Consider, for example, a missive that appeared in *The Toronto Star* in May 1996, which sums up the peculiar fears of these intrepid freedom-fighters. "As an increasing number of people have become more sophisticated," wrote Barry Tait, of Don Mills, Ontario, "they have learned to strip away the left-wing code words/phrases of 'socialize,' 'strategic planning' and 'high quality daycare' and have gained some insight into what the leftist agenda is really about." Tait observes darkly that "'socializing' children via day care and the like is really to create the collectivist mind-set at the earliest possible age so that children will become, later in life, amenable to the dictates from a centralized state authority."

Give us a break, Mr. Tait, and continue your valiant struggles against the socialist hordes elsewhere. Surely, if we have learned anything about early childhood care and education in the last fifty years—and I assure you we have learned a lot—it is that substitute parenting in a safe, well-organized setting not only works just fine, but also has many advantages. There is a wealth of evidence, for example, that children fare much better in school when they have participated in stimulating communal activities in their preschool years, instead of having been parked in front of the television set—the mother of all child-minders—by their parents.

There is a also a wealth of evidence that early-childhood programs such as junior kindergarten pay big dividends in the future. Not only do such programs improve overall school performance in later grades, they also produce children who have an easier time coping with adolescence and early adulthood, and thereby reduce the need for costly remedial services. And, Mr. Tait, you might be interested in the reliable evidence that these programs also turn out children less likely than others to engage in criminal behaviour in the future, less likely to drop out of school, less likely to take drugs, and less likely to require assistance from the state when they grow up. We are making an enormous mistake, says Paul Steinhauer, chief psychiatrist at Toronto's Hospital for Sick Children, when we look only at our economic deficits and ignore the social deficits intertwined with them. "We are going to pay later," Steinhauer warns, "if we allow our kids not to make it today."

All this aside, the majority of Canadian women work—many from necessity, a few from choice, most because they have made a lifestyle decision based on choice *and* necessity. To pretend otherwise, or to think that giving them a small tax credit to stay home will drive them out of the workplace, is absurd. Almost two-thirds of Canadian women with young children are in the paid workforce; more than two million children under age thirteen, half of them under age six, have working mothers. The majority of women, whatever their reasons for doing so, will continue to work in the future, and to think that they will not is to be living in a fantasy world.

Statistics Canada figures show that if women stopped

working in Canada, the number of two-parent families living below the poverty line would increase fourfold, from
the 4 per cent of families currently living in poverty to 16
per cent. The problems this would cause us—in health-
care and welfare costs, to take just two examples—would
be significant. Consider the United States, Mr. Tait, where
widening inequalities of income have led to dramatic
increases in child poverty and created a society in which
one child in four routinely does not receive enough to eat.
Then ask yourself whether this is really what we want for
our children.

Given that women will continue to work, unless they
choose not to, can there be a more important task for our
governments than to find affordable ways to provide children with the very best care when their parents are working? In the process, of course, we might also discuss related
matters—to find ways, for example, to enable women who
wish to do so to take longer paid maternity leaves to stay
home longer with newborns—without undermining efforts
to improve the quality of care and education our children
receive. Instead of draining the system, we should be working within it to create multiple options that meet the needs
of children, of their parents—both parents—and of society
as a whole.

The anti-daycare crusaders seem to have forgotten that
children have fathers, whose lives have changed dramatically in the last three decades too. "As women gain parity as
bread-winners, men gain parity as parents," observed
Margaret Wente, in a *Globe and Mail* column in April 1996.
"Most fathers today are infinitely more involved in the
daily lives of their kids than their own fathers were. They
take turns at everything: the cooking, the bath-time, the
doctors' appointments and the guilt."

As Wente points out, job arrangements today are as var-
ious as child-care arrangements. "Some dads stay at home
or work part-time by choice; some couples both freelance
and take turns minding the kids. Is it easy? No. Do they get

by? Rather well. How do the kids turn out? Many of them are much closer to their parents than my generation ever was." When pollsters have asked women in recent years whether they would choose to work even if they didn't need the money, Wente adds, most women say yes. "And if you could offer them the lives their mothers had, most of them would turn you down."

The subtle, and sometimes not-so-subtle, disinformation campaign against working women organized by conservative organizations such as Real Women and fuelled by well-to-do, right-wing journalists such as Danielle Crittenden and David Frum attracts the usual crowd of reactionary neoconservative malcontents. It also mobilizes people such as Genuis, the Calgary psychologist—and adviser to several provincial governments—who argues that studies indicate that infants and young children in child care for more than twenty hours a week are at risk of having insecure emotional bonds with their parents. Genuis's insistence that a "meta-analysis" of recent studies of non-parental care proves his point so outraged eighteen respected academics from universities across Canada that they released a paper denouncing his views. The academics were concerned not only that Genuis offered no real proof for his theories, but also that the theories were being used by right-wing politicians to legitimize their political ideology and to justify the withdrawal of support for early-childhood programs.

The attack on daycare also attracts men who have always believed, deep down, that women are stealing their jobs. In an economic climate characterized by job loss, scapegoating is endemic, and women take their place with immigrants, minorities, and the devil on the hate list of those who feel hard done by. Yet the proliferation of low-paying service-sector jobs in the nineties—the majority of all new jobs—has *impeded*, not enhanced, many women's opportunities for satisfactory employment, just as it has stalled their opportunities for advancement, and redistributed their wealth.

Statistics Canada figures show that in 1994, women working full-time earned about seventy cents for every dollar earned by men, a marginal increase in the last few years that reflects, in part, a decline in men's average income. But there is a great deal of evidence that women are making little progress towards income equity. A recent study by Queen's University tax expert Kathleen Lahey, for example, found that women receive only about 30 per cent of income from all sources, including government transfers, in Canada, and that their apparent progress in income parity is a cruel illusion.

One way to look at the campaign against women, of course, is to see it simply as a pendulum swinging, a return to traditional notions at a time when our values are changing for many different reasons. But lest we forget how deeply ingrained and how absurd were these notions of the workplace as an exclusively male domain, allow me to quote once again from *Sociology of Occupations and Professions*. This 1971 textbook, aimed at students of sociology in North American institutions of higher learning, was published at a time when more than 40 per cent of North American women were in the paid workforce. Nevertheless, when the book's author, sociologist Ronald Pavalko, asks rhetorically in the introduction to the book, "Why study work?" his answer is "because a substantial part of men's lives are spent in occupational activities."

"Men's work," Pavalko continues, links them with others through work-patterned social interaction. "Men's" occupational roles form the basis of their sense of personal identity, and are an important basis of social integration. There are several other important reasons for studying "the work men do," Pavalko continues. One is that a person's occupation is a very good predictor of many aspects of "his non-work life."

Aside from a brief reference to the socio-economic origins of "girls" who study to become teachers, the only other mention of women I could find in the book is a discussion of "socialization during training periods," which begins: "Up to this point our discussion has dealt largely with research on comparatively prestigious occupations. To avoid the impression that socialization occurs only in occupations of this kind, this section concludes with a discussion of a study of prostitutes—33 call girls—in the Los Angeles area." If this is the world we wish to return to, we're in deep trouble.

Still, old paradigms, although they may lie underground for twenty years, die hard. Recently, in the name of "family values" and under cover of the recession and the changing workplace, there have been vitriolic attacks against working women by neoconservative zealots that would have made most Canadians cringe ten years ago. But now many of us, egged on by right-wing tub-thumpers, aren't so sure. *Are* women taking men's jobs? *Are* women neglecting their children? Perhaps women *can't* cope in the new economy. Perhaps we really should go back to the fifties.

Or perhaps we have the makings of a deal here. When those who would remake society by bribing working mothers to stay home are ready to urge corporate employers to acknowledge that they have abandoned their "traditional" obligations to society, when they are prepared to stop grousing about the Canada Pension Plan and employment insurance and the high taxes corporations have to pay, when they are prepared to urge large employers to stop contracting out jobs, forcing people to work for less money and no benefits, when they are ready to acknowledge that it is impossible for families in most parts of Canada to live comfortably on $35,499 a year—the average annual wage—more working mothers may be prepared to discuss their "anxieties" about daycare. Until then, most of us will continue to believe that the "concerns" of the zealots are tainted by self-interest, self-absorption, and blinkered ideology.

By and large, the harangues of the new right bespeak a mentality—and a line of attack—imported from the United States and described nicely by Susan Faludi in her 1991 book, *Backlash: The Undeclared War Against American Women*: "Behind the news, cheerfully and endlessly repeated, that the struggle for women's rights is won, another message flashes. You may be free and equal now, it says to women, but you have never been more miserable."

According to the "experts," Faludi notes, women are suffering "burn-out." They are succumbing to an "infertility epidemic." They are grieving over a "man shortage." They are crumbling under a "profound crisis of confidence." They are "feeling guilty" about leaving their children. But how is it, she inquires, "that women are supposed to be in so much trouble at the same time they are supposed to be so blessed? If the status of women has never been higher, why is their emotional state so low? If women got what they asked for, what could possibly be the matter now?"

The "matter," Faludi says, is not that women have changed their minds about wanting their place in the workplace on an equal footing with men, or that they are "feeling guilty." Rather, neoconservatives have mounted a "powerful counter-attack on women's rights" in an attempt to retract "the handful of small and hard-won victories" of the last three decades. Just as Reaganism shifted political discourse far to the right and demonized liberalism, she adds, so the backlash has convinced many people—including many women—that women's "liberation" was "the true contemporary American scourge—the source of an endless laundry list of personal, social, and economic problems."

If this is all sounding familiar, it is because such sentiments are part and parcel of the arguments the increasingly noisy anti-daycare activists are disseminating in Canada. The Reform Party, for example, maintains that employment-equity programs give special treatment to women and minorities, thereby discriminating against white males. Similarly, the party recognizes only the "traditional" family, even though StatsCan reports that the two-parent family is in the minority in Canada. The irony is that in the five years since Faludi wrote her book, our faltering economy has done more to damage women's place in the workforce and further the ends of social reactionaries than their own cramped policies, questionable research, and overblown rhetoric.

When did you last hear anyone suggest, for example, that the status of women in Canada has never been higher? When did you last hear anyone suggest that women have gotten everything they asked for? Most Canadians don't believe these things are true. But the Rumpelstiltskins continue to insist that they are, just as many of them insist that most women now realize that they were wrong to want paid employment and equal treatment in the first place.

What most women want today, it seems to me, is exactly what most men want: decent jobs, decent pay, opportunities for advancement, and a measure of respect. In the harsh economic climate of the nineties, however, what many women, like many men, are getting is grief. Not only has the push to greater workplace equality been stalled and discredited as pay- and employment-equity programs have been dismantled or shoved to the back of the queue, but women are also more likely, because of their greater representation in low-paying service-sector jobs, to be displaced by new technologies, or—and this is equally serious—to be devalued by them.

While it is the case that more men than women in Canada have lost their jobs in the nineties, it is also true that most men are in a better position, financially, to cope with job loss. Because their incomes were higher, on average, than women's, they receive more generous severance packages when they are laid off. Similarly, if they belong to an employer-sponsored pension plan and decide to take early retirement, their benefits will be greater because their earnings were higher. Their Canada Pension Plan benefits are likely to be greater, too, not only because their incomes were higher, but also because, unlike many women who leave the workforce for extended periods to raise children, they will have contributed to the plan longer.

Radical changes in the way we work and in the work to be done have also disadvantaged many women who still have jobs. The critical momentum towards workplace equity that had been building over the last three decades has been lost. Similarly, many women have lost opportunities for advancement that once were open to them. As technology alters work, the quality of the jobs in highly feminized workplaces is changing. In financial services, for example, most transaction processing is now fully computerized, and we, as customers, do much of the work that bank employees used to do for us. We become our own tellers every time we use an automated bank machine or a debit card, and our credit cards have turned us into our own loans officers, eliminating jobs.

Moreover, financial institutions, readying themselves for their global forays, are merging and consolidating—and eliminating more jobs, most of them women's jobs. In hospitals, electronic datafiles have eliminated the jobs of people, mostly women, who used to handle everything from patient registration to equipment purchase to inventory, and shifted the work, such as it is, to less-skilled, part-time employees. In retail, salespeople are being replaced by electronic product listings or catalogue telemarketers—increasingly based offshore—as their employers explore ways to eliminate all human contact with their customers. And so on.

Not only has new technology cost many women their jobs, it has also blocked the possibility of their moving up to better—and better-paying—jobs in the course of their working lives. It is also making the jobs they now hold less fulfilling and agreeable. While powerful computers, fabulous software, and lightning-quick, ever-expanding electronic webs of information have opened exciting new worlds to many Canadians—including, of course, many women—the new technologies are at the same time diminishing the working lives of many others.

Information technology divides people into two groups,

a relatively small group of those who control the information, and a much larger group—trapped in isolated, mind-numbing jobs—who are controlled by it. Shoshana Zuboff, in her 1988 book, *In the Age of the Smart Machine: The Future of Work and Power*, describes how this division happens. A factory worker no longer manipulates a sheet of steel. Instead he manipulates data about the steel. A bank worker no longer serves customers and processes cheques. Instead she sits alone in front of a computer screen, manipulating electronic pulses. A supermarket clerk no longer takes inventory. Instead bar codes scanned at the check-out counter become data that automatically trigger a chain of events that require no human facilitation.

Zuboff calls this phenomenon "informating" and she shows how, at each step of these operations, people have lost their jobs because computers are now doing their work. Those who manage to keep their jobs in factories and banks and salesrooms are now required to do boring, repetitive tasks that bear little relationship to the socially interactive work they did before.

Technology has been a mixed blessing for women, and for many men as well. As we shall see in the next chapter, much work that once involved human judgment, intuition, skill, and autonomous decision making has been transformed into passive, repetitive, mindless work in which software does all the thinking. This deterioration in the quality of jobs, many of them in highly feminized occupations—and in women's prospects for advancement—is a far more likely explanation for the frustration many women are feeling today than Danielle Crittenden's notion that millions of Canadian mothers have suddenly been overcome by grief because they must leave their children in the care of others while they are at work.

Her theory leads her to argue that women should stay home to tend to their children, even if that means that their quality of life will be diminished—advice she herself has not followed. A more helpful approach might be to suggest that we, as a society, should resume our interrupted efforts to find ways to ensure that *all* our children are kept safe, healthy, and happy in an economic climate that is demolishing the dreams of so many of their parents. At the same time, we might wish also to consider the measures we might now take—and the decisions we might make with our votes—that would allow those dreams to rise again.

As the miller's daughter looked around the huge room stuffed with straw, she wondered if her mother knew the peril she was in. Impressed though she was by the little man's mastery of the spinning-wheel, she feared that not even he could help her this time. Had she thought more deeply, she might also have considered the possibility that, in truth, the little man never intended to help her at all, but only wished to steal her first-born child.

Part 3

Chapter 7
Vexations of the Information Age

Suddenly the little man appeared. "Give me what you promised," he demanded.

The Queen was filled with horror and offered him all the riches of the kingdom instead.

Let us consider, for a moment, the deal Rumpelstiltskin turned down.

Perhaps he had no need for the riches of the kingdom because he had gold enough.

Or perhaps he cared little for golden treasures, taking his pleasure instead in his reputation as a cunning magician who could spin straw into gold at will.

Perhaps he knew that the straw was not spun into gold at all, but only appeared to be so, and prided himself on his sleight-of-hand.

Perhaps he wished to control the child in order to control the King.

Or perhaps Rumpelstiltskin knew that all the riches of the

kingdom could not compare with the value of a child.
  Imagine that!

"I am optimistic by nature," declares Nicholas Negroponte, the founding director of the Media Lab at the Massachusetts Institute of Technology, in his 1995 bestseller, *Being Digital*. In this paean to the power and goodness of the computer, Negroponte rhapsodizes that as the business world globalizes and the Internet grows we will see "a seamless, digital workplace," in which bits of information will be borderless, "stored and manipulated with absolutely no respect to geopolitical boundaries." Time zones "will probably play a bigger role in the future than trade zones," Negroponte predicts, with software projects "that literally move around the world from east to west on a twenty-four-hour cycle, from person to person or from group to group, one working as the other sleeps."

This transformation, Negroponte acknowledges, will claim many victims, such as "the fifty-year-old steelworker who, unlike his twenty-five-year-old son, has no digital resilience." He also admits, reluctantly, that no matter how smart they are, computers cannot solve the problems of humanity. "Bits are not edible, and in that sense they cannot stop hunger, just as computers are not moral, and they cannot resolve complex issues," Negroponte says. But he insists, in a classic statement of techno-determinism, that the digital age, in which the dominant units of human interaction are bits of electronic information, "cannot be denied or stopped," because "it has four very powerful qualities that will result in its ultimate triumph: decentralizing, globalizing, harmonizing, and empowering."

Few would disagree with Negroponte's assessment of the fundamental ways computers are transforming workplaces around the world, or with his insistence that people must learn to be "digital" if they wish to prosper in the workplaces of the future. But there are many who question his triumphalism, and doubt the validity of his predictions. Indeed, growing numbers of people suspect, deep down, that digital sceptic Clifford Stoll might be closer to the mark when he suggests in *Silicon Snake Oil* that our networked world might not be a "universal doorway" to freedom and prosperity. Might it instead be "a distraction from reality"? Stoll asks. "An ostrich hole to divert our attention and resources from social problems? A misuse of technology that encourages passive rather than active participation?" Computers "don't vex me," Stoll says. "I'm vexed by the culture in which they're enshrined."

A good many Canadians these days share Stoll's vexation with the culture in which technology is enshrined. We love our computers, but we also see them displacing people from their jobs at a breakneck clip. We know the efficiencies computers can effect in our lives, but we are baffled by the insistence of ultra-techno-optimists like Negroponte that it is only the fifty-year-old steelworker who is suffering in the current economy, not his digitally proficient twenty-five-year-old son. We applaud the democratizing, educating, empowering promise of the Internet, and then watch in amazement as it transforms before our eyes into one more way for snake-oil pitchmen to make a buck.

We look at the dismal effects of high unemployment— especially of the astronomically high rates of unemployment among young Canadians—on the social fabric of the nation, and we wonder how long it will be before the short-term pain gives way to the promised long-term gain. We also wonder if Negroponte is correct when he insists that the real division technology has wrought in our lives is not between rich and poor, but between young and old.

Divisions between young and old certainly *do* matter in the nineties, but we question those who see these rifts as little more than perceptual differences in the way people of different ages relate to new technologies. We fear that such simplistic notions are obscuring fundamental issues of workplace equity and distribution of wealth in a society in which the young, for all their facility with digital technology, will be left holding the short end of the fairness stick. Is it possible, we wonder, that bad as it is for the fifty-year-old steelworker, it may be even worse for his son who has the education and ability to get on in the computer world, but who still will find—no matter how often he retrains and reinvents himself—that there is no place for him in the permanent workforce.

Most of all, we wonder how thoroughly Canada must be remade in the likeness of the United States before corporate interests and international investors will be satisfied. ("Canada's fiscal rehabilitation has been breathtaking," crowed a May 1996 *Globe and Mail* editorial, which pointed out that in 1992 total government deficits amounted to 7.4 per cent of the country's gross domestic product—second highest among the G-7 countries. The International Monetary Fund now predicts that by 1997, Canada's total deficits will have plummeted to 1.3 per cent of GDP—the lowest of any G-7 country—and that Canada will be the *only* G-7 country in surplus by the year 2001.

Having got our fiscal house in order, we wonder, what more must we do to please them? Equally important, we wonder what we must do to placate the social reactionaries who have hitched their ideological wagons to the corporate juggernauts of deficit reduction, government bashing, and self-reliance. Why would we wish to do *anything* to placate them, given their dedication to policies that are deeply divisive of Canadian society. Must we accept their efforts to remake Canada according to a narrow, exclusionary, inward-looking vision that seems more appropriate to the nineteenth century than to the twenty-first?

Delegates to the June 1996 Reform Party assembly, for example, described themselves as "outsiders in a corrupt system," blamed the federal government for "the disintegrating family" and Canada's "crime-ridden streets," referred to equity programs as "social engineering," and called Jean Chrétien and the entire Liberal government "crooks"—all the while slagging French Canadians, attacking civil rights, and endorsing a proposal to repeal federal gun-control legislation. Why should the rest of us endeavour to accommodate their vision at all?

It is the meshing of these two agendas—the corporate push to gut social programs and marginalize government in aid of short-term profit, and the neoconservative, social-Darwinist push to gut social programs and marginalize government in the name of morality—that has many Canadians particularly vexed and confused. On the one hand, we desperately want to believe in the promise of the global economy. We want to believe optimists such as Nuala Beck, who in books like *Excelerate* draw detailed road-maps of the future that pinpoint where the "good" jobs will be and how to prepare for them. We want to believe our politicians and corporate leaders, who point out that Canada is exceptionally well placed to thrive in the global economy. We want to believe that our patience with corporate restructuring and our support for government cut-backs will pay big dividends in the future.

At the same time, we see social-assistance programs we knew to be working well vanishing. We see funding for schools and universities evaporating, and support for research and development drying up. We see politicians' vote-getting commitments to job creation and retraining melting away—all in the name of "self-sufficiency," a concept that is less an affirmation of human potential and dignity than a signal that we are on our own in this brave new world, whatever our personal circumstances. We see workplaces in which more and more people are obliged to sacrifice whatever autonomy they once had in their jobs to technologies that simultaneously monitor their performance and control their activities—and, many would say, their minds.

Nowhere is the short-sighted folly of this "ostrich" mentality clearer than in the near-total absence of public discussion about the workplaces of the twenty-first century: What safeguards should we be devising for those permanently swept aside by technological change? What protections should we be putting in place for those who, inevitably, will be victimized by new technologies in the future? Similarly, as regulatory bodies disappear or are privatized—removing checks on the destructive practices of giant corporations—what protections should we be devising for the environment? Although a changing economy offers sparkling opportunities for those equipped to take full advantage of them, many jobs in today's economy are appalling. Indeed, it is likely Canadians will need at least as much protection from exploitation in tomorrow's workplaces as in those of the past.

Our governments, however, are eliminating or severely limiting existing protections that took us years, as a society, to put in place. Workplace-safety legislation has been weakened in many provinces, and funding withdrawn from programs designed to find ways to improve the working lives of the "new reserve army" of temporary and part-time workers. Environmental-safety laws have come under increasing attack from corporate interests, daycare subsidies have been reduced, social-support systems have vanished, and entire programs designed to give temporary assistance to those displaced by workplace change have disappeared. Moreover, new protections that we should be putting into place—right now—to deal with the hazards, indignities, and invasions of privacy of the digital economy have been pushed aside on the excuse that we can't afford them, or don't really need them.

Instead, politicians revive the concept of workfare, an eighteenth-century solution to joblessness that ignores the root causes of unemployment and demonizes its victims. The Ontario Tories, for example, announced in April 1996 that they would spend $100 million—the first instalment on a $500-million election promise—to give unemployed welfare recipients "a hand up" in a community-service-based program called "Ontario Works." They ignored warnings from economists and social-development experts that the programs won't work, and that they will cost considerably more than current provincial welfare expenditures. Indeed, government spokesmen admit that saving money is a secondary consideration to establishing a "principle"—that those who receive assistance from the state should not receive it "for nothing."

They also admit that it would cost less to give more generous tax breaks for charitable donations to agencies that could then create real jobs for those currently receiving assistance. Under the terms of Ontario Works, however, able-bodied welfare recipients—with the sole exception of single parents with children aged three and under—will be required to work seventeen hours each week—just enough to avoid minimum-wage legislation—at tasks determined and overseen by charities, municipal authorities, and non-profit service organizations such as the Rotary Club, and will remain on social-assistance rolls.

As *Globe and Mail* columnist Michael Valpy pointed out in his April 2, 1996, column, many Ontario welfare recipients, "being eager to put distance between themselves and passive income-support and to re-attach themselves to the labour market," voted for the Tories in the hope that the promised workfare program would develop their skills and lead to permanent employment. However, he notes, mandatory workfare is unworkable as a transition program when there are no jobs for participants to move into. "You can't put hundreds of thousands of people instantly into the work force," he points out, "and even if you could, the cost and mechanics of monitoring those people—policing the unwilling—would be prohibitive." Sending welfare recipients to do work that unemployed people would eagerly do for pay in order to stay off welfare, he adds pointedly, is "madness."

The madness of the neoconservative approach to social assistance is that it blames the poor for both their lack of work and their lack of money, a demonizing ethos Canadians have been trying to eradicate for decades.

Doubtless, workfare programs in Ontario and Alberta, and in New Brunswick—which has adopted a kinder, gentler version of the concept that also costs more on a per-job basis than conventional job-training and job-creation programs—will help some people acquire new skills, boost their self-esteem, and eventually enable them to find paid employment, just as the programs will achieve some beneficial results in the way of community services.

That is to the good. But these benefits must be weighed against the paid jobs they will eliminate, the energy they will divert from genuine job-creation initiatives, and the subtle damage they inflict on society by legitimizing a punitive and vengeful assumption that all social-assistance recipients are free-riding shirkers. The benefits must also be evaluated in the absence of proof that workfare can save money, lead to better jobs, create a healthier economy, or foster a more civil society. What leads Canadians to better jobs, as has always been the case, is the existence of better jobs.

In Ontario, United Way officials were so vexed by the workfare program, which depends on the participation of many organizations it funds, that soon after the details of Ontario Works were announced, they wrote to all forty-four regional offices in the province urging them not to get "directly involved" in it. Pressure mounted from unions, who threatened to withdraw funding and support from any agency that supports the "job-killing" initiative, and from social-development groups who view workfare as a damaging, socially regressive measure.

Then, fearing that Ontarians would curtail their charitable giving and create an even greater danger for those in need of assistance, United Way officials backed off, making it clear that they continued to be concerned that welfare recipients will displace paid workers, and that workfare will divert attention from job creation. By its very nature, workfare had created a terrible dilemma for groups such as the United Way, whose mandate it is to help the deserving, not to discourage donations by becoming involved in a bitter political battle.

The unsympathetic ethos that justifies workfare as a means of ensuring that nobody gets a "free ride" smacks of moral hectoring and narrow self-interest. It also bespeaks a stubborn and foolhardy unwillingness on the part of politicians to plan constructively for the future, and fosters a similarly unsympathetic, one might even say hostile, attitude towards efforts to curb exploitation and promote health and safety in the workplace, which come to be seen as a costly indulgence of minor complaints.

If the symptoms of the old industrial economy were bad backs and broken limbs, the symptoms of the new digital economy are boredom, stress, and repetitive-strain syndrome, the malady born of performing mindless tasks over and over again, usually at a computer keyboard. Yet we have all heard people—usually managers whose jobs comprise a variety of daily tasks and human interactions—deny that repetitive-strain syndrome even exists. Secretaries once worked at their typewriters all day, they argue, without complaining that their fingers got tired. These denials are usually accompanied by bitter complaints that company health-care benefits and sick-leave policies are being abused—usually by women—who imagine or exaggerate their afflictions. Yet one massive study, by the U.S. Occupational Safety and Health Administration, found that more than 50 per cent of the U.S. workforce is at risk of repetitive-strain syndrome, numbers that will continue to rise as the numbers of low-level data-processing jobs increase. (Assuming, of course, that all such jobs are not shipped to third-world countries, where the women who fill them work for a pittance.)

It is not much of a leap from blaming the disabled for their disabilities, the unemployed for their lack of work, and the poor for their lack of money to blaming teachers for turning out "products" who are perceived by the corporate community to be "unsuitable" to the workplaces of the global economy. There is something terribly discomfiting, for example, about politicians and corporate leaders whose creative ideas for reforming the education system are for schools to teach only subjects that foster "employability" and to ensure that every student has access to a computer.

Clearly, the ability to use a computer is going to be an important skill for young people to have, both while students and in their working lives. But what, precisely, do these politicians have in mind? one wonders. Do they want children to have access to a computer so that they will learn to think? Or so that they will learn "keyboarding," to be "ready" for the jobs of the future, jobs that will require basic computer skills, but will not require workers educated to think for themselves?

Toronto writer Robert Fulford expressed similar concerns in his commencement address to graduating students at King's College in Halifax in June 1996. Lamenting that "progressive education" has fallen out of favour, Fulford observed that Nicholas Negroponte demonstrated "the new contempt for knowledge at its most preposterous" when he wrote in *Being Digital* that "most American children do not know the difference between the Baltics and the Balkans; or who the Visigoths were, or when Louis XIV lived," and then asked rhetorically, "So what? Why are those so important?" Negroponte, Fulford noted, "believes young people should be taught how to think, a task that will largely be accomplished through computers," yet also "believes apparently that thinking can be fruitfully pursued even when uncoupled from subject matter." "Mr. Negroponte," Fulford added, "appears not to care whether students have anything to think *about*."

Computers do not make people smarter just by being there, and information is not knowledge, Clifford Stoll reminds us. Computer networks "are awash in data," he points out, but only a little of these data comprise information, and only "a smidgen of this information shows up as knowledge." Combined with ideas, some of the information is useful, Stoll observes, *if* it is mixed with "experience, context, compassion, discipline, humor, tolerance, and humility." Perhaps, he adds, knowledge may even, from time to time, become wisdom. But, he cautions, "minds think with ideas, not information," and "no amount of data, bandwidth, or processing power can substitute for inspired thought."

Most Canadians would agree with the proposition that our public schools could generally do a better job of educating our children. As always in a democratic society, debate on how they might go about improving the quality of education is both healthy and necessary. Our problem is that the current push for reform has been driven almost exclusively by the ideological fervour of the corporate lobby and the social Darwinists, to the exclusion of genuine educational considerations and the views of professional educators. In *Class Warfare: The Assault on Canada's Schools*, an alarming analysis of the ideological targets our schools have become, Maude Barlow and Heather-jane Robertson point out that politically motivated reforms, from the right or the left, are dangerous, because they "nearly always flow from simplistic analyses and justifications" and because they invariably, and deliberately, devalue the expertise of professional educators.

Our educators must take some of the blame for the opprobrium heaped on public schools in recent years, Barlow and Robertson observe, because they have been largely "unsuccessful in communicating how the characteristics of schools are interrelated, and how the most well-meaning reforms can set off a chain of unintended and almost irreversible" consequences. Yet, educators have been as intimidated as the rest of us by the ill temper of the times.

In Canada in the nineties, assaults on schools have usually been launched from the right, and our educators have been caught in the same strait-jacket as the rest of us:

diminishing resources and the bullying insistence of deficit-obsessed politicians that "there is no alternative" but to slash budgets, change curricula to please business interests, and accept the view of corporate leaders that schools exist primarily to meet their market-driven needs, not to meet the broader need of society for an educated, independent-thinking citizenry.

All over the world, under the banner of "excellence and competitiveness," corporations are moving aggressively to influence what schools teach and how they teach it, and to imbue classrooms with the ideology of the marketplace. According to the U.S. Consumers' Union, which conducted one of the few major studies of corporate intrusions into public education, more than twenty million U.S. school-children used some form of corporate-sponsored teaching material in their classrooms in 1990. Barlow and Robertson offer compelling evidence that Canadian schools are under an equally ferocious corporate assault that has been aided immeasurably by funding cut-backs. "The visibility of corporations, their philosophies, and their products in Canada's classrooms," they observe, "is in large part the result of relentless downward pressure on budgets." School boards and teachers facing budgetary crises, they point out, are often pathetically grateful for the glossy kits and teaching aids proffered by the corporations.

In order to reach students, Barlow and Robertson note, companies must first get to teachers, and they are doing so in increasingly sophisticated ways. They recount, for example, how, at a "much-hyped—and government- and industry-sponsored—environmental education conference called Eco-Ed," teacher and environmentalist David White "was surrounded by promotions from all the bad boys of the world of industrial pollution and toxicity." Hydro-Québec was there "with its 'polished' environmental ethic; there were two really slick booths from the nuclear industry, and Alcan's display made it appear that it was a recycling company. Who would have guessed that we could learn so much about environmental education from the forest industry?" It is hardly surprising that teachers less well informed than White, particularly those "strapped for time as well as cash," Barlow and Robertson observe, may be willing "to trade a little corporate exposure for an attractively prepackaged lesson plan."

There is no shortage of corporations and industry lobby groups offering such packages, Barlow and Robertson observe, citing a 1991 article for *Canadian Consumer* by Michelle Hibler that lists Esso, Kellogg's, the Canadian Sugar Institute, Abitibi-Price, Shell Oil, Pizza Hut, McDonald's Restaurants, Procter & Gamble, Imperial Oil, MacMillan Bloedel, the Canadian Meat Council, NutraSweet, the Canadian Forestry Association, and the Canadian Soft Drink Association among the many commercial voices already present in Canadian classrooms. "It doesn't take much imagination," they add, "to recreate how the soft-drink manufacturers promote good nutrition. Might the Egg Marketing Board's abundant materials happen to forget to mention cholesterol?"

Just as corporations selling everything from pizza and soft drinks to subtle messages about Canada's "sustainable" natural resources are eager to make their presence known in schools—and, in many cases, to shape the assumptions that drive the curriculum—so the makers of computers and computer software are eager to get their products into classrooms. Clifford Stoll laments the way school authorities in cash-poor school districts in the United States are now having to spend every spare penny to upgrade computer systems "donated" by their manufacturers.

Not only do the systems gobble up education budgets, Stoll says, but they are not very good teachers. The state of North Carolina, he notes, spent $7 million to link sixteen high schools with a fibre-optic network in a much-praised and highly visible experiment. But the system was a bust as a learning tool. One teacher who used it to teach Japanese found that she still couldn't manage a class larger than thirty, that she had no way of teaching brush strokes, that she had great difficulty motivating students—and that by the end of the year half of her students had flunked or dropped out. "And what will happen," Stoll inquires, when the system "needs a teensy 'upgrade,' just to nudge it into the next century?" Canadian environmentalist and teacher David Suzuki puts it even more bluntly. "The cry for computer literacy," he says, has been "one of the biggest cons ever foisted on the school system."

The corporate giants don't limit their efforts to invading the public schools. They also have ideas about how colleges and universities should be administered and funded, about what they should teach and how they should teach it, about what research they should undertake, and about who should profit from the research they sponsor. Universities have long had close, and mutually beneficial, ties with the private sector; but institutions of higher learning conducting themselves as though they were nothing more than corporate research-and-development units would have been dismissed as unacceptable interference as recently as a decade ago. As funding has dwindled, however, many institutions are so strapped for cash that they have been forced to rethink their traditional arm's-length relationship with corporate interests, and go cap in hand for support and advice.

Private-sector support, however, often has a high price. As research becomes "guided" research—structured and paid for by corporate interests—its objectivity is swiftly called into question. When, for example, the pharmaceutical industry funds research on its products, how long will it be before the research is directed by its sponsors, not by the autonomous interests of the researchers. Similarly, as universities become ever more dependent on corporate funding, their governing bodies become ever more influenced by corporate voices and corporate priorities. This subtle but steady process of co-option undermines the independence and cherished freedom of academics to follow their intellects wherever they may lead.

Is it not possible that as corporate spokesmen demand government cuts to university budgets—and higher tuition fees to shift education costs onto the shoulders of students—they are dodging their responsibilities to train Canadians to do the work that needs to be done, work that they admit changes so rapidly that "lifelong learning" will be necessary for the worker of the twenty-first century? Instead of demanding that universities train undergraduates to meet their specifications, corporate strategists might consider using the money saved through technological efficiencies and downsizing to assume responsibility for training and retraining programs. Most, however, continue to concentrate on finding new ways to *shed* such responsibilities—along with such other traditional responsibilities as the provision of decent pension plans, good benefits packages, and a measure of job security.

The corporate response to those who suggest they should take responsibility for training new employees—and perhaps those they are about to fire, as well—is usually a huffy insistence that such programs "don't work." (Strange, isn't it, that apparently workfare, which has many of the same objectives, but is dumped on municipalities and non-profit organizations, "works," but employer-sponsored retraining programs are, by definition, "ineffective.") Instead, the money that could fund such training is channelled into corporate coffers, providing improved earnings for shareholders and, often, lavish remuneration for senior executives.

If current retraining methods "don't work," would it not make sense for large employers to explore ways to create programs that do? If schools and universities can be refocused to meet the needs of corporations, as their spokespersons insist they can, why not refocus corporate training programs as well? (Even the World Economic Forum, a corporate organization, chastises Canada in its most recent report on global competitiveness for "weak" corporate commitment to training.) What, then, is the problem?

"Smart corporations know they have to flatten the organizational pyramid," says demographer and economist David Foot, in *Boom, Bust & Echo: How to Profit from the Coming Demographic Shift*, "but that's not all they should be doing." To make new organizational structures work, Foot advises, a company must also install "a new reward system based on providing challenging opportunities that require re-education and retraining instead of promotions up a ladder than no longer exists." Such a system, in turn, requires a commitment by both employer and employee, Foot says, because "it is futile for a company to flatten its structure and at the same time cut its retraining budget—yet that is exactly what many organizations have done in the 1990s." Moreover, he cautions, it will not suffice simply to send employees on courses. "The best-managed companies," he advises, "understand that retraining must take place on the job, whether through apprenticeship programs, mentoring, or other kinds of training."

The corporate argument that retraining is not the responsibility of employers is based, of course, on profits. To expect employers to provide such programs is tantamount to asking them to raise their own taxes, the argument goes; and despite the public perception, corporations cannot afford to pay more taxes. Corporations have good years and bad years, and they need the profits from the good years to make up for the shortfalls of the bad ones. If governments force them to use their profits to retrain workers, they—and their shareholders—will become skittish about long-term profitability. Eventually they will become *so* skittish that shareholders will stop investing in the company, causing it, in the worst-case scenario, to fold its tents and decamp to somewhere with lower labour costs and overheads.

These are powerful threats, so powerful that few large employers have had to made good on them. But it is not to its credit that the corporate community has shown scant interest in finding a "third path" between their single-minded pursuit of short-term profit and the longer-term needs of society for decent jobs. The good news may be that the private sector's obsession with downsizing—although certainly not its obsession with slashing jobs in the public sector—seems to be waning, as fears of corporate anorexia mount. The bad news is that, with some notable and praise-worthy exceptions, employers seem uninterested in explor-ing creative new ways to address employees' needs and wishes.

Flexible work hours, a concept that enjoyed some popu-larity a decade or so ago, for example, can make life a great deal more enjoyable for large numbers of people—com-muters who would prefer to travel to and from work in off-peak-traffic hours; parents who want to be home when their children return from school; and a variety of those who, for their own reasons, would be happy to share their jobs in order to reduce the time they work. Yet such sensi-ble suggestions, and many more, are ridiculed and shouted down by the bottom-liners who insist that they are too costly. Instead, they move in the opposite direction, demanding that their employees work longer, not shorter, hours.

When Toronto's mayor Barbara Hall suggested at a pub-lic forum on unemployment and poverty held at the city's Daily Bread Food Bank in April 1996 that perhaps it is time to talk seriously about shorter work weeks, she was vigor-ously attacked as naïve by corporate apologists. William Robson, senior economist with the C.D. Howe Institute, told reporters after the meeting that Hall was wrong to sug-gest that shorter work weeks were proving effective in Europe, and criticized her for even suggesting that job shar-ing could ease the plight of the thousands of people in Metropolitan Toronto who regularly require assistance from food banks. Hall stood her ground, commenting that "my vision of a city—where everyone has a job—is going to require us to think differently about work." And, she added pointedly, "I think it's time we started talking about it."

There are many people who think it's about time we started talking about such matters. In the depths of the recession, 800,000 Canadians clocked an average of 8 hours' paid overtime each week—a total of more than 333 million hours in the year. Had just half those hours been converted into full-time jobs, 80,000 unemployed Canadians could have had full-time employment for a full year. Pursuing ways to distribute work more evenly, how-ever, requires time and effort—and a willingness to discuss issues calmly and with our focus on the long term. It also requires the private sector to concede that government could play a critical role in the redistribution of work—for example, by changing provincial and federal labour codes to require that after a specified number of overtime hours, employees be compensated in time off, not money.

It also requires employers to develop reliable ways to measure and quantify what their employees actually *want*—and ways to identify and acknowledge the intangible human qualities that have been ignored in the corporate fixation on short-term profit. The irony is that although human capital is both harder to measure and more specific to a particular enterprise than profit-and-loss statements, it may be the most valuable asset most employers have.

There are impediments to measuring human capital, to be sure, but they are in no way insurmountable. Put simply, taking account of human capital involves reclassifying as assets some expenditures that previously were reported as costs. Training programs cost money, but they also increase a corporation's store of intellectual capital; physical improvements in the workplace cost money, but they also improve efficiency and customer service; a genuine com-mitment to saving—not eliminating—jobs when sales are down, in anticipation of increased sales in the future, costs money, but can improve morale and foster loyalty. That these outcomes are intangible does not mean that they are without value.

These are the kinds of trade-offs that many large corporations have been unwilling to consider in the last few years. Yet when, in an economy that has largely recovered from the recession, corporate leaders complain that people aren't buying their goods or using their services because "consumer confidence" is "irrationally low," might they not ask themselves whether they have contributed to this unfavourable situation by viewing so many of their employees as expendable, and, in the process, scaring the living daylights out of all those fortunate enough to still have jobs?

The hypocrisy of such complaints about flagging consumer confidence is breathtaking. On the one hand, corporate leaders pressure federal politicians to keep inflation low so that high interest rates will attract investors. On the other, they complain bitterly that Canadians are refusing to spend. Might there be a connection? Might it be that Canadians are so frightened of losing their jobs, so frightened of losing their safety net, so frightened that their retirement savings will not see them through, so frightened that their children will be cast-offs in the new economy that their fear has paralysed them?

Could it also be that Canadians, recognizing that the natural riches of the world are not infinite, have come to resent those who would persuade them that they must buy more fripperies? Could it be that the diminished riches of the people—and the rapidly diminishing resources of the planet—have caused us to change? Could it be that unlike Rumpelstiltskin, we have remembered that the riches of the marketplace cannot compare with the value of a child?

Chapter 8
The Value of Work

"Alas," replied the girl, "I must spin this straw into gold before the morning and I do not know how to do it."

"What will you give me," asked the little man, "if I do it for you?"

Let us consider the offer. The miller's daughter knew only that she must spin the straw into gold before morning. She could not know that there would be another room filled with straw, and then another.

Nor could she have known that the little man would raise his price again, and again.

In offering him her jewels, she merely made the best deal she could.

In agreeing that he should have her first-born child, however, she must have believed that she had no other choice.

Did she have a choice? Would the King have carried out his threat to kill her if she did not spin the straw into gold? Or did he merely mean to ensure that she would spin diligently?

> *How, in a peaceful and prosperous kingdom, could such monstrous events unfold? How could a benign and generous King threaten to take the life of a helpless subject? And why did Rumpelstiltskin want her first-born child?*

In 1993, Bob Rae's New Democratic government introduced securities legislation requiring corporations trading on the Ontario Stock Exchange to disclose the compensation awarded each year to their five best-paid executives. Shortly thereafter, Mike Harcourt's New Democratic government in British Columbia followed suit, hoisting another corner of the veil of secrecy that shrouded the riches bestowed by corporate Canada upon its own.

There is little in the institutional life of the nation that Canadians enjoy more than a glimpse into the bank accounts of the rich and famous. The compensation lavished on two high flyers in 1993—Magna International Inc. chairman Frank Stronach, who, with a salary of $2 million plus bonuses totalling $7.3 million, won the grand prize for best overall compensation—and Hollinger, Inc., CEO Conrad Black—who, at $1,568,000, won the award for highest base salary—was reported gleefully in newspapers across the land.

Predictably, some among the first crop of the forcibly disclosed complained bitterly that the release of such information was an unacceptable invasion of their privacy; moreover, they said, it could put them and their families at great personal risk. Others argued, weakly, that nobody, including investors in their companies, would be interested in learning how much they made. Why bother to release such information, they inquired testily, when nobody really cared about it?

The first two lines of defence were not persuasive. The U.S. Securities Exchange Commission has long required executive-pay disclosure—including that awarded executives of Canadian corporations trading on U.S. exchanges—on the sensible grounds that the leaders of publicly traded companies should be accountable to the shareholders who own them. The third seemed to many people to be deeply infused with self-interest and self-delusion. In any event, that argument self-destructed: Investors—especially large, powerful institutional investors—cared a great deal about the rewards corporate leaders were bestowing upon themselves.

So, too, not surprisingly, did other corporate leaders. One effect of the disclosure legislation was the padding of the pay packets of many Canadian senior executives who had learned to their mortification that they were making less than their peers, a humiliation alleviated only by persuading their boards of directors of the injustice of it all. For some, the rules of fair play held that they were right to be aggrieved. Others, however, were forced to call on the goodwill and understanding of the tightly intertwined network of corporate board members who can grant such small favours on the unspoken understanding that one day they will be returned.

The miffed were aided in their quest for justice by intrepid media corporate apologists, who pointed out that senior executives in Canada are grossly underpaid by comparison with their American counterparts. "Despite the impressive number of millionaires among Canadian executives, *Financial Post* reporter Richard Blackwell noted in December 1994, "studies show that when it comes to pay, bosses in this country are slipping compared with those elsewhere." Citing a recent Towers Perrin survey showing that "CEOs of Canadian companies with sales greater than US$250 million are paid an average of US$383,780 a year, less than half what top U.S. executives get at similar-sized companies," Blackwell added that "Canada now ranks 13th world-wide, down from second place in 1990." Pay disclosure itself, Blackwell noted sympathetically, "may help push the Canadian numbers back up in the next few years."

We have now grown accustomed to these annual outings. Outside the corporate community, they hold our attention only when the awards seem ludicrously high or egregiously undeserved—or when they are bestowed on senior bank executives whose institutions are reporting record profits while service charges are proliferating, bank employees are losing their jobs, and the gap between the rate of interest charged on credit-card accounts and that given on savings accounts is believed to be usurious.

Nevertheless, the disclosures are serving many purposes. Not only have they fundamentally altered the relationship among senior executives, their boards of directors, and their shareholders, but they have also shed welcome light on how we value and reward work in Canada in the nineties. As well, they have provided potent ammunition for the critics of corporate compensation practices in the long-overdue and rapidly escalating debate on the unemployment crisis and its relationship, if any, to corporate greed.

The overflowing corporate pay packet is an American phenomenon recently arrived in Canada. In the eighties, high-flying U.S. CEOs were celebrated as folk heroes and compensated accordingly, with remuneration packages rivalling those of rock stars and sports legends. In those heady days, Donald Trump and Lee Iacocca put Canadian wannabes like Robert Campeau to shame. The recession tempered some of the excesses, as corporate profits fell to their lowest levels since the Great Depression. But as the U.S. economy recovered in the early nineties, so did the egos and the bank accounts of the corporate stars. The day after AT&T Corp. eliminated forty thousand jobs in January 1996, its CEO, Robert Allen, was generously rewarded. Stock-market traders, applauding the downsizing, drove up the value of his AT&T shares and options by more than US$5 million, although they later dropped in value when investors decided Allan had gone too far.

By then, mega-rewards had become a Canadian phenomenon too. In 1995, Magna revealed that Stronach, its founder, had banked more than $40.7 million the previous year, a record for incentive pay in Canada. The money included $27.2 million realized from the sale of company stock options granted to Stronach at a time when Magna shares were plummeting in value during the recession.

Stronach's good fortune seemed to many observers to be appropriate; after all, it was his company and he had shouldered most of the risk involved in building it. But they were not so generous in their assessments of others on the disclosure lists who were not founders, or even lifers, but were just passing through the organizations that had rewarded them so lavishly. And what of those handsomely compensated executives whose organizations were losing millions? And those whose companies had tossed hundreds of people out of work? Were their cases different? And, even if they were, was it anybody else's business?

These days, many people are beginning to think that it is. When the president of Loblaws was reported to have received a $1-million bonus on top of a base salary of $1,050,000 as the company was declaring publicly that "reducing labour costs" would be "front and centre in 1996," this didn't look quite right to Tracy Copland-DaRocha of Brampton, Ontario. "Can you just imagine the number of non-management employees who could have their salaries paid out of that $1 million?" she inquired politely in a letter to the editor of *The Financial Post*. "I guess that is just another example of a big corporation taking from the consumers and not giving back," Copland-DaRocha added. "I'd imagine Loblaws will be relying on the government to take care of the jobless employees that they lay off who cannot pay their household expenses," she observed, concluding: "It seems to me Loblaws is in a position to promote job creation in tough times, and I as a consumer would in turn look to support its endeavor."

Canadians are getting even crankier with corporate executives who receive huge compensation packages while their companies are downsizing and foundering simultaneously. "Something is very odd, to say nothing of wrong, when a company loses $29 million, sees its stock drop from a high of $50 to $9, lays off 230 of its 2,000 employees, yet watches its chairman pull down a $500,000 salary, and cash in $12.5 million in stock options," observed Jeffrey Simpson in an April 1996 *Globe and Mail* column.

"The company in question," Simpson added, "is Cott Corp., whose chairman, Gerald Pencer, collected about $13 million for the year ending in January 1995." Cott's executive salary structure illustrates a "disturbing trend in our blessed free market," Simpson observed, "a widening and unfair gap between those who keep rewarding themselves so handsomely at the top and the majority of workers in the private and public sector, whose wages are stagnant or falling." In this "neoconservative age of unfettered worship of the private sector and denigration of the public," he continued, "who is there to raise a peep against corporate power, or at least against the evident propensity of corporate executives to remunerate themselves so handsomely while their companies shed labour and clamp tough wage restrictions on the employees."

In recent years, the peeps raised have been few and far between; but disclosure rules are forcing senior executives to explain the reasons for their windfalls. They are also forcing the compensation committees of their corporate boards to address these matters to justify to their shareholders the philosophy, if any, that informs their pay policies. For many charged with this responsibility, the exercise has been a sobering experience, when they discovered that the compensation they were awarding their senior people had very little to do with much of anything.

A 1995 KPMG study, for example, revealed that 35 to 40 per cent of the 239 TSE 300 companies whose compensation policies and practices their researchers examined showed no apparent correlation between shifts in corporate performance and their managers' pay. It also revealed that half the companies assessed had not attempted to make such a link, and that many top executives had too much say in their own remuneration. Just as in recent years some board members had been stunned to learn that they could be held legally responsible for lack of vigilance in successful lawsuits against the corporations they serve, so were many taken aback by shareholders' allegations that they had shirked their duty by failing to link executive compensation more closely to performance—and by failing to define what constitutes "superior results."

Bonus pay for good work is by no means a new concept, of course. Unions and management have long tussled over across-the-board increases for workers, a standard union equity demand, versus merit pay, a usual managerial demand for flexibility and control. But more sophisticated "quality performance incentives" have become highly attractive to corporate employers, not only as a way to reward productive employees and rebuke those who fail to perform to standard, but also as a justification of the huge bonuses many senior executives are awarded for achieving higher profits, or better returns on investment, or a down-sized workplace, or whatever goal is deemed by sharehold-ers and boards of directors to be especially worthy.

The notion that a successful CEO deserves astronomical over-and-above "pay-at-risk" is often based on the peculiar assessment that competent corporate leaders are as scarce as hens' teeth and therefore worth every penny they earn: In 1996, for the first time in Canada, it was possible to earn more than $1 million, and still not be among the top fifty earners. To employees who have lost their jobs, and to those who are working longer hours on frozen salaries to ensure the organization's profitability, however, such munificence can seem like a slap in the face. It may also, as McGill man-agement expert Henry Mintzberg has observed, go to the wrong guy. "The person who should be rewarded for good results," Mintzberg points out, is usually the person who made the critical decision to expand, or re-structure, or develop a new product line, five or ten years earlier."

As shareholders and boards of directors rewrite the rules of corporate compensation, they are under growing pressure to widen the definition of who "matters" in the corporate contract. Until the seventies, power resided exclusively with company officers and their boards of directors. Then, in the eighties, large institutional investors—pension funds, insurance companies, and the like—began throwing their considerable weight around, demanding a voice in corporate governance, including in such matters as executive compensation. Now, there is a growing sentiment among employee organizations and unions—and among many concerned individuals, such as Tracy Copland-DaRocha— that corporations must abandon their exclusive allegiance to shareholders and the short-term profits they demand in favour of a new model that takes into account all the stakeholders in an organization, including its employees and the consumers who buy its products or services.

The "stakeholder" versus "shareholder" debate is gathering momentum, not only among those directly affected by executive compensation policies but also among community, environmental, and development activists. The latter groups argue that it is essential to the well-being of democratic societies—and perhaps to the survival of the planet itself—that corporations take a broader view of their social responsibilities. For many corporate leaders, however, the issue remains a non-starter.

The crux of their argument is this: Corporations are being pressed to honour their traditional responsibilities— to their employees and to society at large—to the detriment of the shareholders who own them. Given a choice between social responsibility and profit, corporate leaders have no choice. If their enterprises are to prosper in the new economy, their overriding obligation must be to pursue profit for the investors who own them. Society will benefit when that profit translates into jobs.

Ron Gage, chief executive officer at the international accounting firm Ernst & Young, elaborated on the rationale of this position when he was interviewed by *Financial Post* reporter Johanna Powell in April 1996. "If you want to have a strong society and strong social programs, you have to start having a strong economy, and the business sector is where wealth gets created," Gage said. "I think companies are quite properly focussing on wealth creation," he added, because "it's only after the wealth has been created that you can deal with the distribution of it." Jean Monty, CEO at Northern Telecom Ltd. and *Canadian Business*'s CEO of the year in 1996, agrees. "The main focus has to be making money," he told Toronto writer Daniel Stoffman, who profiled him for the magazine. "If you don't focus on making money, you can't serve anybody. Economic progress has to be at the top of the list. If you have economic success, you can take care of employees, and you can take care of the community."

Few would disagree that the *raison d'être* of corporate enterprise is to generate profit. But many would question whether the soothing paternalistic view of corporate executives is justified in the job-killing economy of the mid-nineties. There was a time when paternalism, for better or for worse, was the norm in Canada: Employers accepted their responsibilities to their employees, who, in turn, were loyal—and often grateful—to the corporation. In the nineties, however, many employers are insisting that they owe employees nothing more than a paycheque and vague assurances that sooner or later—when profits are high enough—everything will be all right. In the meantime, everything is not all right, and their efforts to create the perfect conditions for Canada to prosper in the global marketplace are only making them worse.

When corporations take their responsibilities to workers seriously, as does Mr. Monty, who—despite his aggressive rhetoric—leads a company far more progressive than most, their operations thrive. But when corporate leaders simply parrot the rhetoric while jettisoning the responsibilities, as many have done in recent years, can it be any wonder that their motives and ethics are called into question? And when those who talk the talk—and wield the axe—reward themselves handsomely, can it be any wonder that their rosy prognostications are dismissed as self-serving fabrications, and that people come to believe that like the King, whose heart grew greedy at the sight of gold, they will never have profit enough?

One topic in the growing debate on compensation practices and corporate responsibility calls out for more public scrutiny. Business leaders insist that because their corporations have become leaner, meaner, and more accountable to their shareholders in the nineties, so governments must become leaner, meaner, and more accountable to taxpayers by conducting themselves like corporations. This analogy has been instrumental in fanning the flames of anti-government sentiment across the country. In Ontario, for example, massive public-service downsizings between 1992 and 1995 left the province with fewest government employees *per capita*. Yet public-opinion polls showed that when they elected the Harris government in 1995, a majority of Ontarians believed that their provincial civil service was bloated and wasteful, and served little purpose.

Yet this was at a time when Ontario was home to more than 35 per cent of all unemployed Canadians, and social-service organizations were struggling to cope with disruptions that rivalled the depredations of the Great Depression. It is hard to imagine a *worse* time to savage the ranks of social workers, teachers and school support staff, health-care workers, youth counsellors, battered-women's shelter personnel, and all the others whose job it was to mitigate these wrenching dislocations. Yet many Ontarians were convinced that employees on the public payroll—or those supported by public money—were the cause of their problems, and voted in a government committed to radically reducing their numbers, and to radically reducing welfare benefits as well.

To point out that many of these Ontarians have changed

their minds as the consequences of the massive cuts trickle down to their own lives—closing their hospitals; eliminating their school programs; throwing their children, or their parents, or their neighbours out of work—is cold comfort. Many still do not understand that the price they will pay tomorrow for buying into the corporate agenda today is a marked diminution in the quality of their lives and a dashing of their hopes.

Add to that the hypocrisy of politicians who slash and burn with such thoughtless abandon. In April 1996, the Ontario Conservatives, having slashed welfare payments by 21.6 per cent, made much of their reform of the compensation packages of provincial legislature members. After passing legislation abolishing existing MPP pension plans in favour of an RRSP-style plan, eliminating some tax perks, and revamping compensation policies, the Harrisites crowed that they had saved taxpayers about $1.5 million annually. Moreover, no improvements to compensation would even be considered in the future, Finance minister Ernie Eves boasted, until the provincial deficit was eliminated and the budget balanced.

A cynical observer might be forgiven for suggesting that this was a disingenuous promise, given that government deficits, once they are on a downward track, can disappear with breathtaking speed, as Ralph Klein's Conservative government in Alberta discovered to its discomfort in 1995, when the provincial deficit inconveniently vanished before the regressive "reform" program it justified had been fully implemented. That niggle aside, the much-vaunted Ontario legislation did not, in fact, reduce the amount of money MPPs took home each month. On the contrary, in a classic case of creative accounting, it actually *increased* their take-home pay by nearly 5 per cent.

Even more troubling is the mounting evidence that these downsizing provincial governments are making a botch of the job. In early 1995, *The Atlantic Monthly* asked Peter Drucker, the premier strategist of corporate restructuring, to turn his attention to government. Drucker rose to the challenge in *"Really* Restructuring Government," a much-discussed blueprint for reform. In it, he spelled out the critical importance of prioritizing change before undertaking it. Successful rethinking of government programs, he stressed, "will result in a list, with activities and programs that should be strengthened at the top, ones that should be abolished at the bottom, and between them activities that need to be refocused or in which a few hypotheses might be tested." Some programs, he advised, "should be given a grace period of a few years before they are put out of their misery.

"If no rational rethinking of government performance occurs," Drucker warned, "we will in all likelihood do what so many large companies have done—apply the meat-ax and downsize." To proceed indiscriminately, he added, will inevitably "destroy performance, but without decreasing the deficit. In fact, it is predictable that the wrong things will then be cut—the things that perform and should be strengthened." Welfare reform, Drucker warned, is "the prime example" of an area that should be approached cautiously and with sensitivity—advice U.S. politicians rejected in August 1996, when they endorsed a Draconian welfare-reform package that, in essence, makes it a crime to be poor.

Neoconservative governments in Canada in the nineties, by and large, have also ignored such advice. They make lists, to be sure, then they slash away indiscriminately, with little attention to whether a service is working well, and whether its elimination will grievously harm those who lose it. Above all, in the grip of deficit-reduction fever, they have had no truck with grace periods and sensitivity. Instead, they move quickly and ruthlessly, imposing across-the-board budget cuts with little assessment of the effectiveness of programs or prioritizing of their importance.

The federal government has slashed away equally ferociously, often on an across-the-board basis. More than 45,000 federal civil-service jobs have been axed—by mid-

1996, about half of their incumbents had retired, been laid off, or accepted buy-outs; the rest are yet to leave, against their will—and Ottawa's role in funding and overseeing social programs has been greatly diminished. In 1995, the federal contribution to provincial health care, postsecondary education, and social programs was transformed into one $29.3-billion block grant to the provinces—to be applied as they see fit—with the promise of less to come in future years. This abnegation of federal responsibility effectively removes many of the constraints that obliged the provinces to adhere to the national standards that took Canadians nearly a century to assemble. Ottawa is also retreating from its involvement in worker training, tourism and recreation, and mining and forestry, and abandoning its traditional role in maintaining national environmental standards.

This is happening just as most of our politicians have embraced the corporate gospel that a good government must be run exactly like a profitable corporation. It is a questionable proposition at best, in that it ignores one obvious difficulty: that the pay-for-performance model advocated by corporate leaders measures performance in terms of profit. However, equity—not profit—is the object of government. "There is a role in our society for different kinds of organizations and for the different contributions they make in such areas as research, education, and health care," notes Henry Mintzberg in "Managing Government, Governing Management," a much talked about article in the May-June 1996 *Harvard Business Review*. "The capitalism of privately owned corporations has certainly served us well for the distribution of goods and services that are appropriately controlled by open-market forces," he observes. However, he insists, this does not mean that government must become more like business.

"For as long as anyone cares to remember, we have been mired in a debate over the allocation of resources between the so-called private and public sectors," Mintzberg says.

"Whether it is capitalism versus communism, privatization versus nationalization, or the markets of business versus the controls of government, the arguments have always pitted private, independent forces against the public, collective ones." Now, he argues, it is time "to recognize how limited that dichotomy really is.... If we are to manage government properly, then we must learn to govern management."

Business, Mintzberg says, "is in the business of selling us as much as it possibly can, maintaining an arm's-length relationship controlled by the forces of supply and demand." Intelligent buyers, he adds, can beware, and protections are in place for "buyers who cannot beware." But *caveat emptor* is a "dangerous philosophy for health care and other complex professional services," he observes, if only because sellers inevitably know more than buyers, who find out what they need to know with great difficulty. "I am not a mere customer of my government, thank you," Mintzberg adds. "I expect something more than arm's-length trading and something less than the encouragement to consume.... Most important, I am a citizen, with rights that go far beyond those of customers or even clients."

Mintzberg is not alone in his concern that we have ceased to see ourselves as "citizens." Others have noticed that right-wing politicians continually encourage us to think of ourselves as clients or customers of government. They also point out that it is no oversight that Ontario premier Mike Harris, the most outspoken public-sector proponent of running governments as though they were corporations, often comments that his responsibility is to "the taxpayers" of the province—not, as politicians used to say, to "the citizens" of the province. Harris "is by no means alone in his belief that business is superior to government," noted Jeffery Ewener, in *The Toronto Star's* "Friendly Fire" column recently. "As a belief," he added, "it has only one flaw. It's not true." On the contrary, asserts Ewener, "history suggests that Canadian business would be much improved if it were run more like government."

Ewener points out that the construction of the Canadian Pacific Railway, "the settlement of the prairies, the extention of Canada from sea to shining sea, were all the work of the government, through its National Policy, conceived by politicians and run by civil servants." When crises struck, Ewener adds, "the response of Canadian businessmen was an almost universal paralysis. Luckily, the government stepped in and told them what to do. The result was a modern industrial nation and the envy of the world."

Many critics of corporate evangelizing of government have pointed out that their prescriptions for change would be more welcome—and more credible—if their own workplace practices were more thoughtful and humane. "Corporate leaders can continue to insist that globalization, technological displacement of workers and relentless re-engineering in pursuit of competitive advantage are forces of nature whose fury they cannot tame," observed *Report on Business Magazine* editor David Olive in April 1996. "Or they can get ahead of the curve by making job retention, worker retraining and commitment to charitable and social institutions in their communities an integral part of their corporate culture." If they fail to change, Olive admonishes, they soon may be in for a rude surprise.

In the United States, Olive cautions the corporate community, a "revolution" is under way, which holds potentially "ominous consequences" for them. Increasingly, he says, ordinary Americans are coming to believe that "business has not delivered the goods" and their sympathy for the neoconservative agenda is waning fast. "If Big Government was thought to have few fans," Olive observes, "Big Business finds that it has still fewer."

There may be a CEO or two in Canada "under the mistaken impression that only politicians hold office at the pleasure of the community," Olive advises his mainly corporate readership in a courteous understatement of the obvious. He concludes, however, with a stern reminder:

"Capitalism exists by popular consent, and the mindless repetition of efficiency mantras and paeans to 'enhanced shareholder value' will not prevail should the public decide that the economic system no longer operates in its interest."

Olive's alert is aimed, of course, directly at the Rumpelstiltskins—those corporate leaders and politicians who, with their outspoken disciples in business-supported think tanks and in the media, demand that we stay on the road of rapid deficit reduction, radical government downsizing, knee-jerk privatization, and far-reaching deregulation, regardless of their human consequences. Those who, in the name of global competitiveness, would have us plunk every penny of our retirement savings in capital markets, regardless of the considerable risks of doing so; those who continue to insist—even after the massive cost-cuttings of the last few years—that our social programs are too generous, our schools and universities too costly, our unions too powerful, our governments too large; those who insist that corporations owe us nothing at all in return for our allowing them to exist, but instead have the right to seize our children to do their labour at any price they care to pay.

As they attempt to foist U.S. standards and U.S. ideologies on us, the Rumpelstiltskins need to be reminded that despite somewhat lower tax rates and a dramatically lower "official" unemployment rate, the United States is a deplorable model for Canada to emulate. We might also suggest to them that they pay some mind to the abrupt demise of the Republican "Contract with America" and the humiliation of Newt Gingrich, its noisiest and most belligerent advocate.

Progressive forces are on the march south of the border, and Newt Gingrich is now a figure of fun, shunned by those who once embraced him so enthusiastically. The "anxious classes," U.S. secretary of labor Robert Reich's term for middle-class Americans whose real incomes have been frozen or in decline for more than two decades, have had enough. As *Washington Post* columnist E.J. Dionne points out in *They Only Look Dead: Why Progressives Will Dominate the Next Political Era* (possibly the most entertaining book on U.S. politics since his 1992 bestseller, *Why Americans Hate Politics*), the neoconservatives have now demonstrated that they have nothing more to offer the anxious classes—who made them the congressional majority in the 1994 midterm elections—than exhortations to "work harder and lobby for the return of child labor."

The Gingrich view of society—that any act of government is unacceptable—has itself become unacceptable, Dionne suggests, because it rules out assistance from government for Americans making the painful transition into the global economy, and leaves the anxious classes wholly at the mercy of the market. But it is the market, he points out, that made the middle classes anxious in the first place. Now that they realize neoconservatism has moved them "towards a rendezvous with nineteenth-century laissez-faire doctrine," they have lost patience not only with Gingrich and his Contract with America, but also with the corporate interests who view a return to *laissez-faire* capitalism as a necessary condition for global competitiveness.

In their pursuit of profit for the few at the expense of the many, the neoconservatives, Dionne says, have forced their opponents "to grapple with the task of constructing the twenty-first century alternatives to *laissez-faire*." No longer are middle-class Americans prepared to put up with an ideology that "breaks the link between the success of the affluent and the well-being of everyone else." The persistence of Hillary Clinton's communitarian book, *It Takes a Village*, on U.S. bestseller lists—and the spectacular crash and burn of Newt Gingrich's political credibility—suggest that Dionne is right. In the last year, many Republican leaders have distanced themselves from suggestions that America's economic future may be secured by ripping into social programs and slashing welfare, and the Draconian welfare reforms endorsed by the U.S. Congress in July 1996—which effectively criminalized poverty—may well be the last hurrah of the ultra-conservative right.

Even more ominously for Rumpelstiltskins, some mainstream Republicans, although they rejected Pat Buchanan, continue to endorse his fierce attacks on "corporate welfare." (Bob Dole's surprise choice of Jack Kemp as his vice-presidential running-mate simply confirmed the ideological turmoil raging in Republican ranks.) An internal GOP poll undertaken in preparation for the 1996 presidential election showed that as many people were worried about welfare for corporations—about $87 billion a year in the mid-nineties—as were concerned about overly generous welfare for the poor. Many of these people, of course, made up Pat Buchanan's constituency, but many more did not.

More ominously still for Rumpelstiltskins, many critics of the neoconservative agenda are now asking if its policies have created the economic conditions that could lead to a devastating worldwide depression. "During the past decade the one thing Americans have known for sure about the federal budget deficit is that it is bad," began the introduction to a series of cautionary articles on the health of the American—and global—economy in the July 1996 *Atlantic Monthly*. "Government spending soaked up money that industries could have been using to create new technologies. No wonder incomes have grown so slowly; while the American economy as a whole has worn its iron collar of debt.

"But what if the one thing we all know is wrong—or, more precisely, what if it is out of date?" the article queried. In the early eighties, when budget deficits were rising as a share of the national economy, it continued, politicians "were slow to recognize the political and social distortions that a decade of heavy borrowing could create." Since the early nineties, however, "budget deficits have been shrinking in relative and absolute terms." The "broad context"— the current bipartisan drive to eliminate the deficit—is occurring in the midst of falling wages, corporate downsizing, and the Federal Reserve's push for zero inflation, the article added. "The demand-side alternative has no champion in this year's election."

The waning of American prosperity "reflects a shift from the Main Street capitalism of the Golden Age to the Mean Street capitalism of the Leaden Age"—an economic environment that "pits citizen against citizen for the benefit of those who own most of America," observes Thomas Palley, professor of economics at the New School for Social Research, in his article entitled "The Forces Making for an Economic Collapse." The consequences of the shift, Palley says, could be another Great Depression. Low inflation, he warns, means that "were the U.S economy to enter a new recession, it would be likely to experience deflation: prices and wages would actually fall." Were that to happen, "the burden of interest payments on the debts of consumers and businesses would increase enormously, thereby making for a collapse of both consumer spending and capital spending by businesses."

The underlying causes of this dangerous situation, Palley notes, are "the changed conditions associated with the emergence of the Mean Street economy: personal indebtedness and widening income gaps between rich and poor." Debt is being incurred, he points out, simply to maintain living standards. Once households run out of income to service their rising debts, and borrowing stops, he adds, maintaining demand becomes difficult. "Flagging demand for goods and services" in turn causes employers to reduce output and lay off workers, further lowering income and further reducing demand. "These problems would be bad enough in an economy with strong labor unions and low unemployment," Palley warns, "but they are likely to be worsened in an economy in which labor is weak and companies not only lay off workers, but also force wage concessions from those not laid off." These conditions, he adds, are a recipe for disaster.

Does all this matter to Canada's corporate leaders? If it doesn't, it should, for many different reasons. Although Canada is not the United States—which can do pretty well anything it likes with its economy, forcing the rest of the world to adapt and accommodate—it is a made-in-America mentality that has driven reforming, deficit-busting passions in Canada for more than a decade. If the economists most familiar with the workings of that economy now believe that the policies that have governed its economic life since the early eighties were sorely misguided, we would be wise to listen to their reasons. Similarly, because U.S. economic policy inevitably affects Canada, we would be wise to understand the shifts that are taking place there, in order to frame our responses to them.

More important, however, if we pay attention now, we may be able to avoid mistakes made in the United States. Instead of applauding its low unemployment rate—a rate that all objective observers say is grossly underestimated—and envying its pre-eminence in the global economy, we should be thanking our lucky stars that Canadian society has not yet become as deeply divided as American society, and begin talking about how we can ensure that it never does. Although we have walked a long way down the Mean Streets, there is still time to reverse the most socially harmful decisions that our leaders have taken in the last few years. We live in times when once-powerful political parties can virtually disappear in one election campaign. We may also be living in times when once-powerful ideologies can blow away like feathers on the wind. It is, of course, up to us when and how this will happen.

In offering the little man her jewels, the miller's daughter made the best deal she could imagine in the circumstances. In agreeing that he should have her first-born child, she believed that she had no other choice. We, however, know that she did have a choice, had she but realized it. Had she not been all alone in the room, she might have told the little man that his price was too high, that she would not accept his terms. She might have joined with her friends and neighbours to appeal to the King to soften his heart, to regain his senses, to abandon his quest for fool's gold and attend once again to the needs of all his people. In short, she might have told Rumpelstiltskin, and all his friends in high places, to get lost.

Chapter 9
Working Better

"The Devil told you that! The Devil told you that!" the little man cried. In his rage, he plunged his right foot deep into the ground. Then he pulled so hard at his left leg with both his hands that he tore himself in two.

And thus it was that Rumpelstiltskin was no more.

Let us, finally, consider Rumpelstiltskin. A cunning little man, he had everything his own way for most of his story. The King believed that his straw had been spun into gold; the miller believed that he had beguiled the King; the miller's daughter believed that Rumpelstiltskin had saved her from death, little thinking that he would return to claim her first-born child.

Why did he return?

Perhaps he was lonely, and wished the company of the child. Perhaps he truly believed that by controlling the King's child, he could control the King. Perhaps he was a genuinely bad apple, wishing to torture the Queen by taking her first-born.

Or perhaps he was just a shrewd businessman, wishing to complete a deal he had made.

But why did he give the Queen a chance to save her child?

Can there be any other answer than that his conscience, such as it was, obliged him to give her that chance?

Rumpelstiltskin might have stayed away, but he chose to return. He might have seized the child, but he chose to give the Queen three opportunities to name him.

If only he had acted more fully according to his conscience, Rumpelstiltskin might have lived to see a happier day.

Imagine that!

That sympathy for others is the essential characteristic of the human condition was central to Adam Smith's *Theory of Moral Sentiments*, observes John Ralston Saul in *The Unconscious Civilization*, his 1995 Massey Lectures at the University of Toronto; however, this treatise is rarely mentioned by "the false disciples" of Smith's economic theories, Saul notes. Instead, "they limit themselves to a narrow reading of *The Wealth of Nations* and then apply it to the general organization and conditions of society." There is "no indication," he adds, that Smith, who "defined virtue as consisting of three elements: propriety, prudence and benevolence," intended that individuals should apply his free-market theories to their treatment of each other.

By propriety, Saul points out, Smith meant "the appropriate control and directing of our affections"; by prudence, "the judicious pursuit of our private interest"; and, by benevolence, "the exercise of only those affections that encourage the happiness of others." It is hard to imagine, he concludes wryly, "how poor Adam Smith got stuck with disciples like the market economists and the neoconservatives. He is in profound disagreement with their views of society."

Adam Smith is, of course, the eighteenth-century English economist whose dictum, that the market is best left to its own devices to function without interference from government, dominated Western economic thought until the thirties, when the Great Depression proved the argument wanting. He is also the philosophical refuge of those who argue today that government should get off the backs of corporations and out of the lives of Canadians. Yet not only did Smith view human sympathy as among the most honourable of civic virtues, he also had a very dim view of corporations. In *The Wealth of Nations*, which became the fountainhead of neoconservative ideology, Smith portrays corporate entities as suppressing the competitive forces of the market as much as, if not more than, government does.

The idea of benevolence—"the exercise of only those affections that encourage the happiness of others"—matters now, as it did for Adam Smith. The first mark of a Rumpelstiltskin is a refusal to acknowledge that the happiness of others is placed in jeopardy every time an effort is made to force the square peg of unfettered free enterprise into the round hole of the common good. Individuals are not commodities, nor are the purposes and responsibilities of governments the same as those of corporations. To argue that they are—and that therefore governments, like corporations, should be structured to further the pursuit of profit—is to misunderstand the fundamental role of government in a democratic society: ensuring that citizens have substantial authority over the political, civil, economic, and societal forces that determine their daily lives.

In electing the Chrétien Liberals, a majority of Canadians indicated support for a government that would devote its energies to job creation and the protection of Canada's social programs. Instead, they got a government that marginalized defenders of the social-security system and caved in to corporate demands for low inflation at the price of high unemployment. The assault on social programs, undertaken in the name of rapid deficit reduction and at the behest of those promoting the interests of multinational corporations at the expense of those least able to protect themselves politically, bespeaks not only a self-interested want of benevolence, but a dangerously short-sighted vision of Canada's future. The broken promise of job creation bespeaks an equally short-sighted willingness to sacrifice the futures of Canadians to the false promises of the Rumpelstiltskins.

For nearly two decades, Canada, like most of the industrialized countries, has been in the grip of globalization fever, a malady that has distracted us from addressing problems in our communities and has skewed both our values and our actions. Not only has it caused us to wantonly discard many of the attributes that, according to the United Nations, have made Canada the finest country in the world to live in, it has also caused us to abandon our shared efforts to make it even better for those who have not been part of the prosperity, for those who have been treated unjustly, for those whose dreams have been diminished by circumstance or bad fortune.

The corporate community in Canada has a great deal to answer for in this diminution of the dream. When one ideology dominates political discourse—as the tripartite corporate religion of deficit reduction, capital accumulation, and self-reliance has in the nineties—we risk losing the democratic equilibrium that has made Canada a beacon to the world. We also risk not only our first-borns but an entire generation of young Canadians, who face the prospect of falling by the wayside as the rest of us follow our tunnel vision for a global panacea to our problems.

In glorifying the work to be done in the global economy, we have recklessly devalued the work to be done at home. Against all logic, we have told young people that occupations no longer exist, that the career is dead, that no job is worth having unless it involves a joy ride on the information highway. We have devalued the small businesses that provide most of the jobs for young people in Canada by agreeing that unless they aim to be players in the global arena, they cannot—and do not deserve to—thrive.

While it is true that smaller businesses can now accomplish things that only large ones could accomplish a decade ago—just as it is true that physical location is no longer a barrier to doing business around the world—it is not true that businesses serving only local communities no longer matter. Nor is it true that businesses focusing only on Canadian or U.S. markets are engaged in a hopeless enterprise.

Yet, for almost two decades, Canadian politicians, egged on by corporate leaders—and U.S. economists such as Harvard's Michael Porter, who persuaded the Mulroney government in 1991 that Canada's only hope for the future was a single-minded pursuit of "opportunities" in information technologies—have relentlessly chased the global dream. They have devoted both their energies and the country's endangered resources to that pursuit, refusing to acknowledge that many high-tech jobs are not good jobs but mindless jobs that bring with them low pay, no security, and little chance for advancement in workplaces that deny their employees' humanity. Because unemployment has created a buyers' market, these jobs are being filled by people who are overqualified for them—the definition of underemployment—while those who have fewer skills and less education are left out in the cold.

In the nineties, our deficit-slashing politicians have turned their backs on job-creation initiatives—despite their election promises, the federal Liberals have no coherent job-creation strategy—and ignored the need to devise protections for those fated to languish in such jobs all their lives. They have also slashed away at university budgets, cancelled school programs that develop minds rather than skills, and banished what they call "non-essentials"—music programs, art programs, sports programs, and much more—from school curricula. This has forced teachers to instead devote all their energies to preparing students for jobs that don't exist and never will unless we change our ways. Despite countless studies indicating that young

Canadians are willing workers, eager to accept change, corporate leaders criticise and carp, blaming the employment woes of the young on their lack of skills or education or ambition.

The federal Human Resources Development Department has estimated that about half of the jobs created in the nineties will require more than sixteen years of education, compared with only 23 per cent of jobs a decade ago. This means, obviously, that half of the new jobs created will not require postgraduate training. Yet, by denying that these jobs are important—or that they even exist at all—we ignore the needs of those who will find work in traditional occupations, devalue their skills, and abnegate their lives.

It is true today, as it always has been, that countries with the most highly skilled populations have a valuable economic advantage. Canada has such a population. Yet the rhetoric of our global warriors too often suggests that this is not so, that our schools and universities have failed us. Could it be that it is our politicians and global warriors who are failing us? In Ontario, for example, a report leaked to the media by the Ontario Secondary School Principals' Council in April 1996 showed that cuts planned by the Harris government would mean that high-school students would lose 190 hours of core English, math, and science instruction, and would be able to earn up to 40 per cent of their course credits in summer jobs.

The elimination of core educational programs in favour of soft credits for "job experience" would make no sense even if there were a surfeit of jobs available for young people, which there is not. Not only does it devalue the programs being axed by deeming them dispensable, it also flies in the face of abundant evidence that we should be striving to strengthen our schools, not striving to undermine them by slashing their budgets, downsizing their academic and support staffs, and bad-mouthing every extracurricular program that focuses on something other than computer skills.

The late social historian Christopher Lasch warned that a

dangerous psychotic delusion—the need to escape into a fantasy world in which disembodied intelligence can transcend human limitations—lies at the heart of the modern cult of technology. One needn't go that far—although many would agree with Lasch's pessimistic assessment of the digital revolution—to see that we are in grave danger of allowing techno-determinism to overwhelm us as we prepare ourselves for the next millennium. Despite the hopes and promises of politicians and corporate leaders, in the last five years alone Canadians' standard of living has dropped by 3 per cent, the result of downsizings, wage take-backs, and gutted benefits programs undertaken in the name of global competitiveness.

More than a million and a half Canadians are officially out of work. Another half million or more are no longer included in the unemployment tally because they have given up looking for a job. Thousands of people—especially young people—who want full-time work have settled for part-time or temporary work; thousands more are self-employed "consultants," many of them downsized professionals trying to eke out a living. Overall, about 7 per cent of the entire Canadian workforce would like to be working more than they are now.

Is it not now time to consider whether we may all have been too quick to accept the proposition that technology cannot be denied, too quick to accept the Rumpelstiltskins' claim that "there is no alternative." Is it not also time to face the fact squarely that many of us have been accomplices in the Rumpelstiltskins' quest for power and profit. After all, we elected the politicians whose commitment to diminishing the powers of government in aid of loosening the reins on free enterprise has led to the dismantling of the unique social contract that made Canada's humane and orderly society the envy of the world.

Many of us, of course, bought into the neoconservative agenda because it was to our financial advantage to do so. The wealthiest Canadians have much to gain in the world of the corporate free-marketeers. They profit when interest rates are kept artificially high, while those who must borrow suffer. Some of us bought in because we were deeply dissatisfied with the existing state of our governments, both federal and provincial, believing them—often rightly—to be wasteful and inefficient. Indeed, the true genius of the Rumpelstiltskins was their ability to transform our legitimate dissatisfactions with government inefficiencies into a hatred of government itself.

Tom Walkom, in a June 1996 column in *The Toronto Star*, wrote perceptively about how the Ontario Tories under Mike Harris succeeded in turning this trick. Under previous Tory, Liberal, and New Democratic governments, Walkom points out, "it was assumed that government actions, such as regulation and even ownership, gave room for the public interest to flourish." That assumption, Walkom says, is no more. "Harris has replaced the notion of the public with that of the taxpayer." While "the public" may possess interests that clash with those of private enterprise—interests that may, for example, require government to regulate industrial pollution, Walkom observes—"the taxpayer does not. His only interest is in paying less."

If you doubt Walkom's analysis, listen carefully to the words of neoconservative politicians such as Harris and Preston Manning. Hear how the words "citizen" and "society" and "public interest" have been banished from their vocabularies. Hear how negative their appeal is, how dedicated to tearing down what Canadians have taken the better part of a century to build. Hear how divisive it is, how narrow, how mean-spirited. Hear how it assumes that we, as citizens, are mere taxpaying patsies, and how our social programs are nothing more than an attempt by greedy governments to pick our pockets. Listen for a reference to the public good, an acknowledgment that we are citizens first and taxpayers second, a word about how our tax dollars have provided us with a peaceful, prosperous, and tolerant society.

Underpinning this pinched and ungenerous vision are the false assertions of the corporate community that the global economy is the only real economy. The article of faith among corporate leaders—that we now live in a borderless world—implies that national borders are irrelevant. Yet there is no reason to embrace their faith to the exclusion of local economies. As Bruce Little pointed out in *The Globe and Mail's* "Amazing Facts" column in October 1995, data compiled by University of British Columbia economist John Helliwell shows that if differences in size and distance are cancelled out, Canadians trade twenty times as much with each other as with Americans.

In a "truly borderless world," Little noted, Canada's east–west trade would be about 10 per cent of its north–south trade." However, that was not the case, he noted, "even in the 1990s when a weak Canadian economy dampened internal trade while a stronger U.S. economy pumped up Canada–U.S. trade substantially." In 1989, Little added, "east–west trade amounted to 105 per cent of north–south trade for the country as a whole and 128 per cent for Quebec." Five years later, "the figures were 55 per cent and 62 per cent, down from 1989," but still substantial.

A subsequent study by Helliwell, and Royal Bank chief economist John McCallum, confirmed these results and prompted its authors to caution Canadians that "it's far too early" to conclude that the shifting ratio represents the beginning of a new long-term trend. "Especially in the world of management gurus," they warn, "it has become fashionable to speak of borderless worlds, implying that national borders no longer matter for trade and capital movements.... Our work proves that this emerging conventional wisdom is drastically wrong. East–West trade in Canada remains profoundly important." (It would be even more beneficial if provincial politicians could bring themselfs to agree that is time to have free trade within Canada. The Canadian Manufacturers Association has estimated that inter-provincial trade barriers cost the average family of four $1,000 on goods and services.)

To point out the falsehoods disseminated by corporate lobby groups is in no way to deny that new technologies enable governments to operate more cost-effectively, nor is it to deny that government operations and expenditures ought to be tightly monitored and continuously reassessed to ensure that our taxes are spent wisely and efficiently. All bureaucracies—especially publicly funded bureaucracies—drift towards bloat if they are not held strictly accountable for their decisions and their expenditures, just as any government or public institution may become wasteful and duplicative if not held to high standards of accountability.

Nor is it to say that we, as Canadians, have not been living beyond our means for a very long time, demanding more from our governments than we are prepared to pay for with our taxes. Neither is it to deny that Canada faces serious problems as we move from being a country with one of the youngest populations in the Western industrialized world to one among the oldest. As our population ages, most of the demands on government for health care and income support will come from older Canadians, like me. And we will, of course, carry political power with us as we age, because we are so numerous. Projecting the number of retired Canadians who will vote in 2020, compared with the number of young people who will cast their votes, is a sobering exercise.

It is also reason to change our ways before it is too late. Clearly, we, as a society, are not going to be able to provide all retired baby-boomers with the benefits they have been promised without severely compromising the investments we must make in the young. A national budget devoted exclusively to pensions and health care, with nothing left over for research and development, education, and infrastructure, is no way to protect Canada's future, just as allowing 15 per cent of young Canadians to be jobless is reckless folly.

These are hard truths with unpleasant implications. U.S.

economist Lester Thurow points out bluntly that "if you do something for the health care of 20-year-olds, you're investing in the economy, because if you can keep them healthy, they will in fact have long working lifetimes." If, however, "you do something for the health care of 70-year-olds, you're not investing in the economy [because] a 70-year-old's health is pure consumption." Not only must ageing societies such as the United States and Canada face such realities, Thurow argues, but the young *must* be protected by the old—at their expense—because the young will be in no position to protect themselves.

In the United States, Thurow observes, the issue is not poverty. Elderly Americans—like older Canadians—have a *per capita* income substantially above that of the average person under age sixty-five. Retired Americans get back all the money they paid into the Social Security system, plus interest, in less than four years, he notes, and "after that they are essentially on welfare." This means that "poorer people are taxed in order to give money to richer people" in an intergenerational transfer of wealth that severely penalizes the young. "We should set up a system," Thurow advises, under which no one receiving social assistance "gets less than the poverty line, but nobody gets more than the median income"; if individuals want to do better than that, they will have to rely on personal savings and private pensions. "Unfortunately," he adds pointedly, "politicians don't want to face up to this problem because there are so many elderly voters."

Nor, of course, do wealthy Canadians wish to dwell on statistics showing that they, like most large corporations, have prospered disproportionately in the nineties, despite the recession. They prefer to tell us that we are spending too much on the young, too much on the sick, too much on the poor—and that basic-income-security programs are no longer viable because they are too expensive and will harm the young Canadians who will be obliged to pay for them. Might they not also consider that there are other sources of revenue that could put things right—including their own wealth and the wealth of corporations? Instead, they demand tax cuts of greatest benefit to the rich, on the pretext that a few extra dollars in the pockets of middle- and working-class Canadians will create economic growth and thereby benefit all Canadians, including the poor.

If we are wise, we will stop talking about tax breaks that help the well-to-do and begin considering inheritance taxes and higher taxes on corporate earnings. But we are living in a society in which the wealthy have opted out of social responsibility, justifying their actions by insisting that "there is no alternative" and that short-term pain will inevitably bring long-term gain for all. We need now to move beyond the rhetoric of deficit reduction and face the reality of income distribution: the widening income gap in Canada between rich and poor.

The intergenerational transfer of wealth, Lester Thurow points out, is tremendously difficult to deal with in the nineties because it raises new issues not just for North Americans but for humanity. Around 2025, the United States will become the first society in history to be dominated by elderly voters. (Canada will follow shortly thereafter.) Canada is not the United States, nor are our problems identical. But Thurow's warning is as valid here as it is south of the border. If we cannot, as a society, find ways to redistribute our wealth more equitably, we truly will doom an entire generation.

We have twenty years to do this. As demographer David Foot has said, there is no better time to reform Canada's retirement and income-distribution system than now. At the turn of the century, only 13 per cent of Canada's population will be age sixty-five or older. The first wave of baby-boomers won't turn sixty-five until 2012; and the rush to retirement won't end until 2031, when the last of the boomers retire—if they can afford to do so.

If we start now, we can find ways to organize the distribution of work in ways that will ensure that all

Canadians—not just the well-to-do—will have some control over their working lives and a measure of security in retirement. Yet, we are paralysed by corporate arguments that we must work longer, not shorter, hours; that the Canada Pension Plan is unsustainable and employers should not be obliged to contribute to it; that corporations cannot afford to pay more taxes; that it is not the responsibility of large employers to create jobs for Canadians and retrain those whose skills no longer serve their needs. Bah, humbug, and for shame.

In May 1996, *The Economist*, which in corporate circles is always right, presented its readers with an alarmed analysis of why Bob Dole was not going to be the next president of the United States. Noting with pride that Republicans had forced Bill Clinton "to swing to the right," the article despaired of Dole's chances of victory—barring a fatal wound inflicted on Clinton by Whitewater prosecutors—and bemoaned the fact that Dole was in danger of bringing the Republican-controlled Congress crashing down with him.

"Mr. Clinton's instinct," the article warned darkly, "is to meddle and intervene." His plans to "kick-start" the economy have so far been stopped by the Federal Reserve's Alan Greenspan, a Republican, and by his own "worldly" treasury secretary, Robert Rubin, *The Economist* noted with satisfaction. However, "Clinton's meddling inclinations have not yet been tamed," *The Economist* warned. "Interventionist ideas keep flowing," most recently in the president's efforts to "encourage good corporate behaviour." That flow, the unsigned article declared sternly, "must be dammed."

Well, there it is in a nutshell. *The Economist*—and the global warriors who swear by it—think that corporate good behaviour is not to be "encouraged." The rest of us can only shake our heads in bewilderment and despair.

"Capitalism," Lester Thurow reminds us, arose when "a timely ideology"—a stress on maximizing the welfare of individuals—"fortuitously merged" with the new technology of the steam engine, technology capable of driving an entire industrial system. Today, however, Thurow points out, technologies such as computing that rely on human brain power rather than on rich natural resources require a different ideology altogether, an ideology "that fosters collaboration on crucial social investments such as education and research and development."

We now need systematic public efforts to guarantee full employment and develop industries on the cutting edge, he warns, not narrow, self-serving approaches that seek to "dam the flow" of interventionist ideas. We now need to turn our backs on survival-of-the-fittest capitalism, and embrace "a thoughtful mixture of public and private initiative essential to creating an economy that works." We should be endeavouring, in short, to do what Canadians had always done so successfully until the untimely coincidence of a surge of neoconservatism and a wave of deficit fever swept us away into a never-never land in which the rich get richer, the poor get poorer, and one in three young Canadians never gets a chance.

In the last decade or so, Canadians have been denied the opportunity to engage in calm, thoughtful—and genuinely inclusive—discussions of how best to solve the workplace problems that confront us now and those that will confront us in the twenty-first century. In accepting the proposition that market forces alone should determine the way we live our lives and organize our society, we have also accepted the proposition that there is really nothing to discuss. Instead, we have agreed that government must withdraw from our lives, and that we must look after our own interests as best we can. We have accepted that a market left to its own devices can be trusted to provide us with a sound economy and a sound future—an outcome even Adam Smith dismissed as improbable. It is time to recognize the neoconservative cant that the best government is no government for what it is: a concerted attack by the affluent on the unfortunate and afflicted.

William Bridges, a global-economy optimist, reminds us in *Job Shift* that we stand at a watershed comparable to the great shift in North Americans' perceptions of work after the Industrial Revolution plunged them into the urbanized, commercialized, manufacturing-centred world of jobs. "Again the future looks both dangerous and uncertain," Bridges observes. "Again we can see the shadowy outlines of the new post-job world, and again we are unsure that we can deal with the new life that faces us." And what do we do? he asks. "We fight bitterly over the remaining pieces of the work world. We idealize the world of jobs and conveniently forget how boring and depressing most people found it. We forget how unfairly it treated women and minorities and how seldom its promises of success were actually fulfilled with promotion to the top of the heap."

And, of course, he is right. There is nothing to be gained from romanticizing the past. True, we were making progress in ensuring that every Canadian would be treated fairly in the workplace and that each of us would be rewarded, not according to background, or gender, or "connections," but according to how well we do our jobs. It is also true that we still had miles to go before reaching the goals that we have now been obliged to abandon.

What Bridges fails to mention is that towards the end of the nineteenth century, a remarkable thing happened. The citizens of industrialized countries realized that they did not like the direction in which their societies were heading. Suddenly, everything began to change. Child-labour laws were introduced, unions challenged the power and prerogatives of robber barons, workplaces were made safer, compensation was made fairer, pension and benefit plans were created, and employers came to realize that their profits depended upon those who laboured on their behalf.

If you doubt such monumental changes can happen quickly, you might recall that little more than five years ago, the Western world was fighting the Cold War, convinced that the enemy was the Soviet Union. Today, with the Soviet Union no more, we are realizing that poverty, and hunger, and injustice, and environmental catastrophe are the real enemies. These enemies are lurking in our communities, not only in the impoverished nations of the developing world.

The economic future of Canada lies in the success of its businesses—*all* its businesses, large and small. In the next century, they will still be a fundamental social institution, affecting all our lives, shaping our workplaces, determining how most of us work, how much we earn, how we will fare in life. The rapid growth of new, entrepreneurial companies—and the revitalization of older, established corporations—will have impact on all our lives, providing new opportunities to increase the value of our skills. But the health of our society depends on us. If we are duly vigilant as citizens, we will expect our politicians—and our corporate leaders—to take into account the greater good of the society in which they operate.

We will also support our local businesses and those employers who have not abandoned their responsibilities to their employees and to the society in which they operate. Corporate leaders who are prepared to meet these challenges deserve our support. Our loyalty—and the loyalty of their employees—will reward them.

It is now time to tell Rumpelstiltskin that we know his name and that we are not going to allow him to bully us any longer. Nor are we going to accept his terms. Perhaps, however, in honour of Adam Smith and his vision of the prudent and benevolent society, we could make him an offer, something along the lines of "We have named you. Now, we will allow you to participate in our society if you will refrain from demanding our first-borns—and if you will cease your efforts to remake our just and peaceable kingdom in your own image."

Selected Bibliography

Andersen Consulting. *Vision 2000: The Transformation of Banking.* Chicago, 1991.

Atkinson, Michael M., and William D. Coleman. *The State, Business, and Industrial Change in Canada.* Toronto: University of Toronto Press, 1989.

Attali, Jacques. *Millennium: Winners and Losers in the Coming World Order.* New York: Random House, 1991.

Baptista, Joao, and Dwight Gertz. *Grow to Be Great: Breaking the Downsizing Cycle.* New York: Free Press, 1995.

Barlow, Maude, and Heather-jane Robertson. *Class Warfare: The Assault on Canada's Schools.* Toronto: Key Porter, 1994.

Barlow, Maude, and Bruce Campbell. *Straight Through the Heart.* Toronto: 1995.

Barnet, Richard J., and John Cavanagh. *Global Dreams: Imperial Corporations and the New World Order.* New York: Simon & Schuster, 1994.

Beach, Charles, and George Slotsie. "Are We Becoming Two Societies?" Toronto: The C.D. Howe Institute, March 1996.

Beauchesne, Eric. "Pension Outlook Not as Grim as Ottawa Claimed in Report." *The Toronto Star*, September 18, 1995.

Beck, Nuala. *Excelerate: Growing in the New Economy*. Toronto: HarperCollins, 1995.

Bello, Walden, with Shea Cunningham and Bill Rau. *Dark Victory: The United States, Structural Adjustment, and Global Poverty*. Oakland, CA: Institute for Food and Development Policy, 1994.

Betcherman, Gordon. "The Canadian Workplace in Transition." Presentation to the "Managing the Changing Workplace" Seminar, University of Toronto, January 1995.

Betcherman, Gordon, Kathryn McMullen, Norm Leckie, and Christina Caron. *The Canadian Workplace in Transition: The Final Report of the Human Resource Management Project*. Kingston: Industrial Relations Press, Queen's University, 1994.

Bridges, William. *Job Shift: How to Prosper in a Workplace without Jobs*. Reading, Mass.: Addison-Wesley, 1994.

Camp, Dalton. "The Downsized Are Starting to Size Up Their Situation." *The Toronto Star*, May 1, 1996

Canadian Broadcasting Corporation. *Ideas*, "Debating the Welfare State, William Kristol and Bob Rae." April 12, 1996

Canadian Teachers' Federation. *Education and Teachers in the Canadian Economy*. Ottawa, 1993.

Child Poverty Action Group. "Campaign 2000: Child Poverty in Canada, Report Card 1993." Ottawa: Canadian Council on Social Development, 1993.

Corcoran, Terence. "No Mystery to Job Creation." *The Globe and Mail*, April 2, 1996.

Coyne, Andrew. "Let's Create a Nation of Savers." *The Globe and Mail*, August 17, 1994.

———. "Toward a Renewed Pension System." *The Globe and Mail*, March 11, 1995.

Crittenden, Danielle. "The Mother of All Problems." *Saturday Night*, April 1996.

Dionne, E.L. *They Only Look Dead: Why Progressives Will Dominate the Next Political Era*. New York: Simon & Schuster, 1996.

Drucker, Peter. *The Age of Discontinuity*. New York: Harper & Row, 1968.

———. *Managing in Turbulent Times*. New York: Harper & Row, 1980.

———. *Post-Capitalist Society*. New York: HarperCollins, 1993.

———. "*Really* Reinventing Government." *The Atlantic Monthly*, February 1995.

Economic Council of Canada. "A Lot to Learn: Education and Training in Canada." 1992.

The Economist. "Sexual Speculations." April 10–17, 1996.

———. "How Bob Dole Should Fight." May 18–24, 1996.

Ellul, Jacques. *The New Demons*. London: Mobray, 1976.

Faludi, Susan. *Backlash: The Undeclared War Against American Women*. New York: Crown, 1991.

Finlayson, Ann. *Whose Money Is It Anyway: The Showdown on Pensions*. Toronto: Viking, 1988.

Finlayson, Ann, and Sandra Martin. *Card Tricks: Bankers, Boomers and the Explosion of Plastic Credit*. Toronto: Viking, 1993.

Foot, David K., with Daniel Stoffman. *Boom, Bust & Echo: How to Profit from the Coming Demographic Shift*. Toronto: Macfarlane Walter & Ross, 1996.

Francis, Diane. *Controlling Interest: Who Owns Canada?* Toronto: Macmillan, 1986.

Franklin, Ursula M. *The Real World of Technology*. Toronto: Anansi, 1990.

Freeman, Alan. "Canada Pension Plan Going Broke." *The Globe and Mail*, February 25, 1995.

Fukayama, Francis. "The End of History." *The National Interest* Summer, 1989.

———. "The Sober Compromise." *The Times Literary Supplement*, May 10, 1996.

Fulford, Robert. "Elite, the New Scare Word." *The Globe and Mail*, June 8, 1996.

Galbraith, John Kenneth. *The Good Society: A Humane Agenda*. Boston: Houghton-Mifflin, 1996.

Geddes, John. "Business Holds Up Its Side of the Job Bargain with Ottawa." *The Financial Post*, May 14, 1996.

Gee, Marcus. "Apocalypse Deferred: The End Isn't Nigh." *The Globe and Mail*, April 9, 1994.

"General Social Survey and Household Facilities and Equipment Survey." Ottawa: Statistics Canada, 1995.

Genuis, Mark L. "Dr. Genuis Replies." *The Globe and Mail*, August 10, 1996

Girard, Daniel. "New Crunch for Ontario Looms after Job Cuts." *The Toronto Star*, April 12, 1996.

Grant, George. *Technology and Empire*. Toronto: Anansi, 1969.

Gray, John. *Enlightenment's Wake*. London: Routledge, 1996.

Hammer, Michael, and James Champy. *Re-engineering the Corporation: A Manifesto for Business Revolution*. New York: HarperCollins, 1993.

Harrison, Trevor, and Gordon Laxer, eds. *The Trojan Horse, Alberta and the Future of Canada*, Calgary: Black Rose, 1995.

Hellyer, Paul. *Jobs for All: Capitalism on Trial*. Toronto: Methuen, 1984.

Hitchens, Christopher. "Nerd-World Leaders." *The Times Literary Supplement*, May 10, 1996.

Information Highway Advisory Council. *Connection, Community, Content: The Challenge of the Information Highway*. Ottawa: Supply and Services Canada, 1995.

Kanter, Rosabeth Moss. *When Giants Learn to Dance*. New York: Simon & Schuster, 1989.

Kennedy, Paul. *Preparing for the 21st Century*. New York: Random House, 1993.

Kettle, John. "The Shrinking Work Week." *The Globe and Mail*, April 26, 1996.

Kierans, Eric, and Walter Stewart. *Wrong End of the Rainbow: The Collapse of Free Enterprise in Canada*. Toronto: Collins, 1988.

Kingwell, Mark. *Dreams of Millennium: Report from a Culture on the Brink*. Toronto: Viking, 1996.

Kinross, Louise. "Boom Times Seen for Industry." *The Financial Post*, April 12, 1996.

Korten, David C. *When Corporations Rule the World*. West Hartford, Conn: Kumarian, 1995.

Krugman, Paul. Peddling Prosperity: *Economic Sense and Nonsense in the Age of Diminished Expectations*. New York: Norton, 1994.

"Labour Market Analysis Data." Ottawa: Statistics Canada (Analytical Studies Branch), 1994.

Lapham, Lewis. *Money and Class in America: Notes and Observations on the Civil Religion*. New York: Random House, 1988.

Lasch, Christopher. *The Revolt of the Elites and the Betrayal of Democracy.* New York: Norton, 1995.

Levine, Robert A. "The Economic Consequences of Mr. Clinton." *The Atlantic Monthly,* July 1996.

Little, Bruce. "How the West Has Won the Jobs Race." *The Globe and Mail,* May 13, 1996.

Lottor, Mark, and John Quartermain. "Surveyors of Cyberspace." *Internet World,* June 1996.

Lowe, Graham. "The Future of Work: Implications for Unions." The Larry Sefton Memorial Lecture, University of Toronto, March 27, 1996.

Lowe, Graham, and Harvey Krahn. "Computer Skills and Use among High School and University Graduates." *Canadian Public Policy* 15/2 (June 1989).

Luttwak, Edward. "Turbo-Charged Capitalism and Its Consequences." *The London Review of Books,* November 2, 1995.

McLuhan, Marshall. *Understanding Media: The Extensions of Man.* New York: McGraw-Hill, 1964.

McQuaig, Linda. *Behind Closed Doors: How the Rich Won Control of Canada's Tax System ... and Got Richer.* Toronto: Viking, 1987.

————. *Shooting the Hippo: Death by Deficit and Other Canadian Myths.* Toronto: Viking, 1995.

Menzies, Heather. *Whose Brave New World? The Information Highway and the New Economy.* Toronto: Between the Lines, 1996.

Mintzberg, Henry. "Managing Government, Governing Management." *Harvard Business Review,* May–June 1996.

Morissette, R., John Myles, and G. Picot. "What Is Happening to Earnings Inequality in Canada?" Ottawa: Statistics Canada (Analytical Studies Branch, Business and Labour Market Analysis Group), 1992.

Morissette, R., and Deborah Santer. "What Is Happening to Weekly Hours Worked in Canada?" Ottawa: Statistics Canada (Business and Labour Market Analysis Branch), 1994.

Myles, John, G. Picot, and Ted Wannell. "Wages and Jobs in the 1980s: Changing Youth Wages and the Declining Middle." Ottawa: Statistics Canada (Social and Economic Studies Division), 1988.

Naisbett, John. *Global Paradox.* New York: Avon, 1994.

Negroponte, Nicholas. *Being Digital.* New York: Knopf, 1995.

Nikiforuk, Andrew. *School's Out: The Catastrophe in Public Education and What We Can Do About It.* Toronto: Macfarlane, Walter and Ross, 1993.

Noble, David. *Progress without People: New Technology, Unemployment, and the Message of Resistance.* Toronto: Between the Lines, 1995.

Olive, David. "Right Makes Fright." *Report on Business Magazine*, April 1996.

Palley, Thomas J. "The Forces Making for an Economic Collapse." *The Atlantic Monthly*, July 1996.

Pavalko, Ronald M. *Sociology of Occupations and Professions.* Itasca, Ill.: F.E. Peacock, 1971.

Philp, Margaret. "Influential Child-Care Adviser Under Fire." *The Globe and Mail*, April 27, 1996

Postman, Neil, and Charles Weingartner. *Teaching as a Subversive Activity.* New York: Delacorte, 1969.

Privacy Commissioner. *Annual Report 1995-96.* Ottawa: July 1996.

Reich, Robert. *The Work of Nations: Preparing Ourselves for 21st Century Capitalism.* New York: Random House, 1992.

———. *The Next American Frontier: A Provocative Program for Economic Renewal.* Toronto: Penguin, 1984.

Rifkin, Jeremy. *The End of Work.* New York: G.P. Putnam, 1995.

Robertson, Heather. "A Passionate Call to Rescue the Nation." *The Globe and Mail*, October 7, 1995.

Saul, John Ralston. "Language and Lying." *Queen's Quarterly* 102 (Winter 1995).

———. *The Unconscious Civilization.* Toronto: Anansi, 1995.

Schor, Juliet B. *The Overworked Americans: The Unexpected Decline of Leisure.* New York: Basic Books, 1991.

Senker, Peter. "Technological Change and the Future of Work." In *Information Technology and Society: A Reader*, edited by Geoff Einon, Nick Heap, Hughie Mackay, Robin Mason, and Ray Thomas. London: The Open University, 1995.

Shribman, David. "A New War on Corporate Welfare." *The Economist*, November 27, 1995.

Smith, Adam. *An Inquiry into the Nature and the Wealth of Nations.* London: Penguin Classics, 1986

Stewart, Thomas A. "Taking on the Last Bureaucracy." *Fortune*, April 13, 1996.

Stoffman, Daniel. "Mr. Clean." *Canadian Business*, June 1996.

Stoll, Clifford. *Silicon Snake Oil: Second Thoughts on the Information Highway.* New York: Doubleday, 1995.

Sullivan, William M. "The Politics of Meaning as a Challenge to Neocapitalism." *Tikkun*, May/June 1996.

Swift, Jamie. *Wheel of Fortune: Work and Life in the Age of Falling Expectations.* Toronto: Between the Lines, 1995.

Tait, Barrie. "Family Unit in Lib-Left's Way." *The Toronto Star*, May 1, 1996.

Thorsell, William. "Inflation Phobia Leads to Unnecessary Caps on Economic Growth." *The Globe and Mail*, April 13, 1996.

Thurow, Lester. "Investing in the Building Blocks of a Healthy Economy." *Technology Review*, May/June 1996.

Valpy, Michel. "Enter the Era of Mandatory Workforce." *The Globe and Mail*, June 13, 1996.

Walkom, Tom. "Salary 'Cut' Gives More to MPPs." *The Toronto Star*, June 8, 1996.

Wallerstein, Immanuel. *After Liberalism.* New York: New Press, 1996.

"Women in the Labour Force." Ottawa: Statistics Canada (Housing, Family and Social Statistics Division), 1994.

Women's Bureau, Human Resources Development Canada. *Women and Economic Restructuring: Report of the Committee on Women and Economic Restructuring.* Ottawa: Canadian Labour Market and Productivity Centre, 1994.

Wysocki, Bernard. "The Danger of Stretching Too Far." *The Wall Street Journal*, August 11, 1995.

Zuboff, Shoshana. *In the Age of the Smart Machine: The Future of Work and Power.* New York: Basic Books, 1988.

Index